BLACK COOL
ONE THOUSAND STREAMS
OF BLACKNESS

BLACK
COOL
ONE
THOUSAND
STREAMS
OF
BLACKNESS

EDITED
BY
REBECCA
WALKER

SOFT SKULL PRESS | BERKELEY

AN IMPRINT OF COUNTERPOINT

Library of Congress Cataloging-in-Publication Data is available.

ISBN: 978-159376-417-3

Cover design by Matt Dorfman

Printed in the United States of America

SOFT SKULL PRESS
An Imprint of COUNTERPOINT
1919 Fifth Street
Berkeley, CA 94710
www.softskull.com

Distributed by Publishers Group West

10 9 8 7 6 5 4 3 2 1

for Sylvia Ardyn Boone (1941–1993)
& Robert Farris Thompson

who taught me what I knew to be true

CONTENTS

FOREWORD
HENRY LOUIS GATES, JR.

There are 40 million black people in this country, and there are 40 million ways to be black. Some might take this claim of radical individuality as somewhat naïve. The Princeton scholar Eddie S. Glaude, Jr. points out that such a formulation runs the risk of being a little too easy (he called similar thinking "pimply faced" in a recent lecture), in that it addresses the lives of black persons, but not of the black *people*.

When I gesture toward the myriad ways to be black, to act black, to feel black, I do not mean to suggest that we are all of us in our own separate boxes, that one black life bears no relation to another. Of course not. We are not a monolith, but we *are* a community. And the members of a community talk to each other—and talk about each other.

This book that Rebecca Walker has so creatively put together, *Black Cool: One Thousand Streams of Blackness*, is a compelling and sustained conversation about the multiple meanings of blackness in the United States today. In this brilliantly conceived and edited volume, we see a multiplicity of ways in which blackness is both definitive and interpretive, confining and liberating, imposed and embraced, perceived and, even at times, ignored. The essays in this volume encourage us to hold two seemingly contradictory ideas in our minds at once: On the one hand, blacks as a group share culture, language, and experience that join us inextricably together, but as individuals, we may well act in our own self-interest, without regard to the needs of "the community."

In other words, it is a simple fact that sometimes we define ourselves in terms of each other, and sometimes we do not. The seminal essays in this volume show us, in careful and thoughtful detail, that it remains necessary and productive for African Americans to have a continuing conversation about this simple fact. This is a superbly edited collection, and constitutes a major contribution to our understanding of what we might think of as the fundamental problem for African Americans in the twenty-first century: how class differentials within "the race" compound individual experiences of anti-black racism, and ever more profoundly shape what it means to be "black" itself.

INTRODUCTION
REBECCA
WALKER

This book began to write itself many years ago, when I was a student at Yale and had the good fortune to study with three extraordinary human beings: art historian and anthropologist Sylvia Ardyn Boone, cultural critic and feminist icon bell hooks, and Robert Farris Thompson, a pioneer who has spent his life identifying, cataloguing, and excavating what we now call the Afro-Atlantic aesthetic tradition.

I grew up around this tradition. The mark of Africa was always in our home, mediated through the African-American artistic lens in photographs, books of poetry and prose, my mother's garden, and the music of Stevie Wonder and John Coltrane. But even as a young girl, certain things held my eye longer than others; some objects demanded to be touched, held, examined, apprehended with greater care than others.

There were chairs. In almost every room, my mother left a seat, a potential throne, open, and waiting for a visitor to come, human or spirit, whatever shape or form. There were even pictures of chairs—in my mother's study, a Modigliani painting of a girl in a tall chair watched from above her desk. On the wall in the hallway, another painting of a chair: empty, red. In the living room, a long wooden bench of walnut, an old church pew. Leaving a space for spirit: a trope of West African ritual.

Quilts were carefully spread over beds in our house, and often admired for their design, color, or size of stitch. Intricate composition and surprising use of color held the cultural recognition of the value of cloth, the wealth that is both beauty and dowry, but also screamed the signature of the artist, who, through audacious aesthetic choices, asserted a profound authenticity and thus resistance to all that would rob her of subjectivity. As in many examples of African art, patterns often featured the zag, the break, chevron-like symbols that seemed to come directly from the cloths of West African art.

At my uncle's home, cars filled the driveway, and sometimes the front yard, too. In West Africa, the Yoruba worship Ogun, the god of iron and war. In antebellum America, enslaved Africans were known for their blacksmithing skills, and forced to forge the iron of their own shackles because of it. In contemporary African-America, isn't a reverence for metal, that which comes from the very core of the earth and represents strength in the face of all obstacles, visible in the driveways of my uncles?

At my grandmother's house in rural Georgia, family photos spread like kudzu to cover the wall above her favorite chair in her living room. This massive display was nothing less than a symbolic manifestation of the power of kin.

And then there was the bath. While my mother or I soaked, the other would sit on the floor alongside the tub and tell the news of the day. After, coconut oils and amber potions were sampled, and more talking. Looking at our reflections in the mirror, laughing and sharing thoughts, my mother and I birthed ways to see the world and our places in it; we grew through those conversations, we became.

Like the Mende women Sylvia Boone so lovingly describes in her book *Radiance from the Waters*, my mother and I entered the space of cleansing waters and emerged renewed and radiant. *Neku*, the Mende call it. Beautiful. Fresh.

Cool.

I did not question these objects and rituals, or the others that marked our days, until I began to study art and aesthetics three thousand miles away from home, inside of cold, neo-gothic buildings stripped bare of color and heated with hard radiators that burned my fingers when I reached out to them for warmth. I knew then I had been in the presence of something else before I arrived in that icy city, which both fed my mind and chipped away at my spirit.

When I began to study with Boone, Thompson, and hooks, I learned in words what I had only known in feeling. They spoke of *the other place*, the other language I had left behind. Through their work, these teachers taught me that the language of my home came from a people whose names had been erased, whose tongues had been cut from their mouths, whose traditions had been deemed punishable by death. But, these teachers said, those people had not surrendered because their code was so deeply embedded in them, the specific contours of their humanness could not be vanquished.

My uncles taught me about heaps of metal that could take me where I needed to go. My grandmother's wall demanded I pay attention to ancestry, kin. The quilts taught me how to put shards, remains, and scraps of both the material and psychic worlds together to make myself a shield, a protective coat of arms. My mother taught me how to enter the bath an ordinary woman, and emerge a queen.

I began to see the fingerprints of Africa everywhere.

I was captivated in the same way by an image of President Obama during the election season of 2008. Once I put it on my wall and continued to look, this book continued to call itself into being, to knock on the door of my studio and demand to take its place in the empty chair I leave, always, beside my desk.

You have seen the picture. In it, Obama emerges from a sleek, black Town Car wearing dark sunglasses, a suit, and a red tie. That is all, and yet, in this picture, Obama is indisputably cool. He is so, so cool I cannot turn away from the image. I want almost to eat the image, to ingest the cool, but what I really want to know is *what makes him so cool* in this picture. I want to know if that ineffable quality can be decoded, understood as the sum of its parts.

I want to know this because I am inexplicably drawn to it. Because I have had this feeling before, and intuitively sense there is something going on in this picture that is distinctly Black, and I want, *I need*, to know what. And so I begin to take the picture apart, to see through it. I absorb, in some place behind my eyes but not quite in my brain, the elements that rivet. I mediate. I translate. I follow in the footsteps of my teachers, and I start to see:

Barack Obama emerges from the metal of a shiny black car as the Mende would emerge from the bath: fresh, new. No longer a boy with big ears, he steps out a prince, a relative of Ogun, the heir apparent. He is in motion; his body exits the automobile in the shape of a Z; he is propelled by what seems an unstoppable force. He wants to taste this new experience, this new life; he reaches powerfully, for what is yet unknown. Obama is set to be our first black, our first mixed race, our first Muslim-named president. His family is intact and shiny, his wife and children jaw-droppingly beautiful. His audacity is astounding. His reserve is mesmerizing. His swagger is undeniable. His family is unbreakable, and full of soul.

The Cool in this photo is so palpable it sends a shiver up my spine. It is Black Cool. It is made up of elements that can be traced back to a place, a people, and a culture, elements brilliant writers take on in this book. In these pages, Michaela angela Davis says Black people own this cool, and should not give it up for pennies on the dollar. I say Black Cool can be shared, but its genus cannot be forgotten, cannot be erased again. Can Black Cool be tried on, adapted, assimilated, co-opted? Yes. Can its birthplace be denied? Only by those invested in gratuitous erasure. And these writers, and this editor, are not.

Read this book. Contemplate it. And add your own elements to the collection that's here—there are many more than what you'll find in these pages. Hybridity. Fluidity. Harmonious dissonance. But those are for you to discover, dear reader. To see, know, and honor as you wish.

Let us build a periodic table of Black Cool, element by element. Let it grow like kudzu, denying all that would deny it, and moving at speeds so lightning fast, it cannot, ever, be stopped.

BLACK COOL
ONE THOUSAND STREAMS
OF BLACKNESS

AUDACITY
dream hampton

My rape story makes me feel guilty. I will tell it as simply as I can.

I was an eighth grader, a "senior" at a magnet middle school for "gifted" children. In the way that children who display academic aptitude are plucked from their neighborhood schools, I was separated from mine, and from my school-aged neighbors, and bused less than three miles away from an increasingly rough neighborhood. I was born on Mack and Helen, on Detroit's "Black Bottom," a notorious and working-poor neighborhood that had become synonymous with urban blight by the mid-twentieth century. My mother and stepfather moved a few inches farther east, to the lower half of a two-family flat on Eastlawn and Charlevoix, where as a kindergartner I was once pummeled by much older boys with snowballs stuffed with rocks.

There were seventies gangs in my neighborhoods whose fifties-style monikers belied their menace: the Bubble Gum

Gang and the citywide-famous Errol Flynns. By six, I preferred to read than to go outside. "Outside" was confrontation masked as "playing"—mean talk meant to carry on the tradition of signifying, but these dozens had become a bit meaner, more misogynistic. As a post toddler, I didn't have the language to describe this misogyny; I knew only that being called a "yellow heifer," when all I wanted to do was learn to double Dutch, hurt my feelings. Then there was the uneasy way sexual attention from grown men made me feel.

There was one group in particular, who posted up on the Vatican-style wall meant to protect the Polish Catholic church that served free summer lunches. When groups of tiny girls walked by, these guys would comment on a pair of nipples that wanted to sprout or on what would a decade later be a round ass. If you weren't lucky enough to be in a group larger than three, these twentysomething men would reach right out and "smooch" our booties, "smooching" being a euphemism for sexual harassment by pedophiles. The boys our age would watch and learn and chase us down on the playground and try and smooch our booties. Or drag us out of sight and dry-hump us or, worse, tear our panties down and show their friends. I'd like to say this wasn't most of the boys, but it was. It was the few boys who didn't play that way—like my friend Junior, whom the other boys called a fag—whom I remember most.

Junior heroically got socked in the eye, dragging a much older girl (she was a second grader, we were still in kindergarten) away from a group of boys. When he told the teacher, and then the principal, what had happened, he was threatened so badly by the boys and men in our neighborhood that he and his mom left our block. I was so sad the day his grandmother came and put eleven black garbage bags, containing all of their belongings, into her wood-paneled station wagon. I avoided the playground from then on. Became a teacher's pet. Spent lunch hour organizing and cleaning the room.

Then my mother and stepfather moved me and my brother a mile north, past Chandler Park Drive, to a neighborhood that was made affordable to my waitress mom and mechanic stepdad because of sudden white flight. My parents bought a gray brick three-bedroom house with a pool from a white family running to Adrian, Michigan (a neighborhood that would in a decade become all Mexican—I imagine that family ran again). Having an aboveground pool that was six feet deep in the center was a huge deal. My brother and I leveraged our access to chlorinated water to make friends in our new neighborhood, which to us felt damn near upper middle class. I was a better swimmer than my brother and most of the boys he befriended, but it didn't stop me from nearly drowning the time three boys held me underwater trying to remove my bikini top. I remember being humiliated at the time.

When my top was finally removed, there wasn't much to see. I was seven. Still, I internalized the attack and sat in our kitchen nook, watching the boys bully my brother in our own backyard, taking over our pool almost ten at a time. At night, I'd sneak into the pool and float on my back and count stars.

I'd dream I was queen of my pool, but, more important, that I alone had dominion over my body. I'd stare at the moon till my fingers pruned, but always, after the attack on my halter bikini, in a one-piece racer-style swimsuit. Or sometimes shorts and a long tee.

As in my old neighborhood, my fear of "outside" was widely understood as my being "stuck up" and "light-skinned." When I did come out to play, few of my friends found my interests interesting. I liked to tag and describe rocks and soil, read science fiction, and drum the theme song to *The Six Million Dollar Man* on empty chlorine pails. I was never great at double Dutch, or backward skating. I did excel at jacks, and would always have a set and a ball handy in my pocket should one of the girls on my block be interested. Sometimes they wanted to play; most times they ignored me.

And so it went. I wasn't the loneliest girl in my city, but I probably believed I was. By third grade I began to understand my mother to be an alcoholic. In the Pisces way, this was mostly an act of self-harm. Having drunk a bottle of vodka, she'd be passed out on the couch by the time we got home from school. My brother saw it as an opportunity to steal money from her purse to go to the arcade. I saw it as an opportunity to clean.

It wasn't until the summer before fourth grade that I discovered I was fearless. My "real" father, who was always present, had given me and my brother a matching pair of green and yellow

Schwinns. The boys on the block knocked my brother, who is 363 days younger than I am, off his bike and called it their own. My brother came home bloodied, muddied, and crying. I put down my book (I distinctly remember I was reading Madeleine L'Engle's *A Wrinkle In Time*), went to the backyard, where my own bike was chained to the fence, unlocked my bike, put the chain around my neck, and rode around the corner to get my brother's bike. When I got around the corner, three boys were arguing about who was going to ride my brother's bike next. I hopped off my own, and it fell to the ground on my friend Marqueila's grass. I told them to give me the damn bike.

It was my first time cursing to anyone but my mirror. The boys laughed at me. I took the bike chain from around my neck and swung it at the legs of the boy trying to mount my brother's bike. He fell to the ground in pain, and the group's leader, Marvel, an older, fifth-grade boy who'd already grown taller than my mother, pushed the bike my way, holding the other two boys back from revenge as I walked our twin Schwinns home around the corner. I remember being surprised at my lack of adrenaline rush (I'd learned about such things watching the Bionic Man). My heart wasn't beating fast at all, and what I remember most is how deeply annoyed I was that my book had been interrupted. My diary entry from that night says as much.

By fifth grade I learned I loved to drive. I'd steal my mother's car as she was passed out on the couch, stack some books on the driver's seat, and circle my neighborhood with one arm out the window, like I'd seen my father do. In my mind, my neighbors were duly impressed. By middle school my writing skills had become public knowledge, and boys at my neighborhood junior high, Alexander Hamilton, would pay me their lunch money to write their essays. Some of these boys were as old as fourteen and had mopeds. My friend Darius had a red moped and a chin-length jheri curl and had been held back once. He really wanted to make it to high school, so I began doing all his homework, and when he ran out of money I'd barter rides on the back of his moped. He'd take me back to my old neighborhood, which had only become worse in the three or four years since we moved, and I would watch kids and young men who dressed alike battle-dance each other doing elaborate pop-and-lock routines.

Darius was the big brother I never had. He'd remind lecherous high school dropouts that I was only eleven ("She ain't even got no titties, man!"), backing them off me when they'd try to talk to and touch me. I was losing my fear of "outside."

My seventh-grade English teacher nominated me for the highly selective magnet school Bates Academy, where I'd graduate from eighth grade. In the spring of my second semester at my new school, Marvel and two boys broke into my house to rape me. It was storming that night. A movie kind of storm. My mom was waitressing nights and my stepdad often stopped at a bar near his job before coming home. I'd cooked dinner for my brother and his friend Bo. Or, rather,

I'd shaken some drumsticks in a Shake 'n Bake bag and roasted them in the oven, then chopped some carrots and poured Italian dressing over them and fed my brother and Bo, who was from the block where the boys who'd stolen my brother's bike lived.

I was in my bedroom on the second floor when the doorbell rang. Bo was in the bedroom attached to my room, a room that had once belonged to my parents but now, since they'd moved to the basement for privacy, was called the "playroom," where they'd left a bed, a TV, and a chair. Bo was sitting on the chair, watching TV. The bell rang more than once, and I went downstairs to see if my stepdad had lost his house key. He had not. Marvel and two other tall boys were yelling through our heavy wooden locked door, through the thunder and the rain, for my brother to open up. I told my brother he better not even think of it. My brother looked at me, on the stairs, and then again through the window, where Marvel was threatening his life should he not open the door, and he did something that still makes my heart sink: He opened the door and let the outside in.

The three boys, who were all older than sixteen (I'd learn this later, from Friend of the Court documents), pushed my brother aside the moment he cracked the door and chased me upstairs, where I was hoping to lock myself in my room and use the fire escape ladder my dad had bought me to run to my neighbor Ms. Erma's, across the street. I remember having that plan in my head. But they ran faster than I did. And were stronger. And they threw me on the bed in the playroom, where Bo sat frozen, and pulled off my panties. There was an attempt, many attempts, to pin me down, to keep my legs from kicking, but I would not stop kicking. I kicked and I punched and I screamed and I spat and I squirmed.

One of the teenagers pulled his penis out; it was my first time seeing a real one since I'd bathed with my brother as a preschooler. I kicked the boy in his groin and he doubled over, just like in the movies. One of the other boys slapped me, and for a moment I didn't fight. Then Marvel pulled out his penis and I regained my fight. I wanted to will myself into the Tasmanian devil, to be un-pin-downable, impenetrable. And I succeeded.

After what was more than fifteen minutes, what felt like much longer than the second half of *The Brady Bunch*— which, once the police came, was how I measured the time— the three boys finally gave up. One of them said, "She don't wanna fuck." And they left. My brother never came upstairs to help. Bo never left the chair where he sat in the same room the entire time.

I've told this story three times. To my two best friends and to a lover I trust. In the sister circle where I sit, or the many friendships where my girlfriends have asked me to witness the telling of their own rape stories, I've stayed silent. I always feared my not being raped because I refused to stop fighting would seem an indictment of their stories. But I don't feel that way. I don't believe they weren't strong enough or should have fought if they didn't or that their rapes were in any way their fault. But I never tell my own story, because of a kind of survivor's guilt. That, and the deep contempt I hold for Bo and my brother.

But now, here, I see it all differently. Now I know I tapped into something bigger than me. My audacity is my fight, to be bigger than my fear. I've never been able to summon fearlessness by anger, even when it's been a reaction to deep injustice, social or personal; instead it's functioned in my life as a kind of walking meditation, one that has driven me around the world and back. That stormy night on the east side of Detroit was terrifying, but it was also the night I learned there's nothing I fear too much to fight.

THE
GEEK
MAT
JOHNSON

Look, let's get this out of the way right now: Geeks are not dorks. Dorky, sure, but that's not the definer. *Dorks*: socially awkward, stumbling into a constant patina of embarrassment. Merriam-Webster lists its definition only as "nerd; also jerk," but it is a combination of the two. The dictionary goes on to describe a geek as "one who is perceived to be overly obsessed with one or more things including those of intellectuality, electronics, etc.," but that's only halfway there.

No, the defining element of geekdom is an overwhelming *passion* for the idiosyncratic intellectual crush. It could be on computers, comic books, much maligned or obscure fantasy movies. The crush could be international politics or third-world finance, or the history of forgotten or imagined continents. The subject itself doesn't matter—that doesn't define the geek. The passion for that crush object does. An interest so large it at times blots out the existence of the rest of the world.

Geekery uses passion as a passport, a transportation device to take you to a different world: a land of your choosing.

I'm a Black geek. A comic-book geek, specifically. When I refused to pick up *Snow, Snow* by Dr. Seuss one more time to try and push through the words, my mother decided it might be better to have me start on *The Incredible Hulk* instead. I've been geekily passionate about comics ever since.

The store that sold them in my neighborhood in Philadelphia was down the block, past a corner where the local society of future violent offenders would congregate, but I didn't care. I would hustle through them anyway, just to get my fix. The covers were ripped off so the store could sell the books for just a quarter, but I didn't mind. I loved what was on the pages. In comics, good and evil were clearly marked; the good always won, and the weak were always protected. As a boy being raised solely by my mother, I instinctively knew I was missing a world of men, and that's where I found them, on those magical pages.

I didn't let anyone outside my house know about my passion for comics, though. Books, even comic books, were not acceptable in my larger environment. I grew up going to a public grade school where it was a lot easier to get punched in the face than it was to learn anything. By second grade I'd figured out that a good way to stay safe was to not stand out, not break from the herd, lest the predators notice me and pick me off. My cousin Alex was three grades ahead of me, and just as nerdy as I was. I looked up to him, in part because he was proof I could survive three years down the line.

One day on the schoolyard, I saw Alex walking around with his head stuck in a magazine. Immediately, I ran over to see what it was, because the only magazines I'd seen kids bring to school were nudie magazines and I just knew I was going to get to see an image of fully developed mammaries. One of the thug kids saw the magazine, too, and saw me running and joined in behind me.

When we got there, I asked, "What you reading?"

Alex, annoyed, held up the cover for me to see: the *Economist*. The Negro was reading the *Economist*, right there on the do-or-die lot of Henry H. Houston Elementary. The thug who had followed me pulled it out of Alex's hands, flipped through the whole thing, and said, "It ain't got no kind of pictures. What? You just reading to read?" and threw it back. I like the news, my cousin told him. The thug looked at Alex like he'd lost his gottdamn mind. He left Alex alone after that, because he thought Alex really had. And Alex kept reading, cool as ever. Confident, relaxed, like he already knew he was going to end up sitting in a corner office as a millionaire tech CEO and the thug was destined to sit on a bed in a Pennsylvania State Correctional Institution. Which is what happened.

It wasn't just that Alex was reading, or what he was reading, either. It was what he was saying: *I'm smart*. In a playground filled with boys who were trying to prove their worth by being the best at handball, or dunking the basketball, or slashing the third-grade teacher's tires, or seeing who could convince a girl to throw her better judgment, Alex was just saying, *I am smart*. And therein lies the heart of black-geek coolness. The center of its power: *I know more than you, and knowledge is power. You do the math.*

Even during slavery, black intelligence was reluctantly acknowledged. It had to be: Those who ignored the ability of the people they were subjugating did so at their own great risk. For slave owners, the risk of underestimating a slave could result in loss of their human property, or even their own lives. But with a belief system of Black inferiority, that acknowledgment had to find ways of expressing itself in coded language that didn't challenge white supremacy. Runaway-slave notices, which depended on detailed written descriptions of the slaves themselves in lieu of pictures to identify the fugitives, often referred to the bright runaways as "cunning" or "artful."

We see the intellectual ghost of this tradition of backhanded, evasive acknowledgment of Black aptitude today every time a Black artist or athlete is referred to as a "natural" or a "talent," as if he were just born supremely capable, cut off from the effort and brilliance it takes to develop greatness. In response, the black geek wears his intelligence like a feather boa at a gay pride parade—and with similar dimensions of defiance of cultural expectations.

Blackness is one of the few identities that comes with its own self-enforced expectation of expression. Why are you listening to chamber quartets? That's not Black. You're learning Greek? What kind of Negro learns Greek? Camping? Black people don't go camping. You're a Buddhist? You need to get your black ass to church. Blackness can be a rigid, didactic identity, with people stepping out of line facing ridicule and admonishment or, worse, condemnation. Those who reject the perceived identity of Blackness can be seen as rejecting the whole of black worth itself. They become perceived as sellouts, or self-hating bigots, whose goals are to advance by cutting loose from the group.

African American identity was forged in an environment of the external violence of white supremacy. Everything African was belittled, devalued, demonized, disregarded. In response to such a climate, identity had to be rigid or it would be useless. Identity in this situation became armor, hard and unbending, protecting those who wore it from being defined by those who would do so to destroy them. The race war is largely over, or at least on the wane, and without that change in social climate the black-geek aesthetic couldn't exist. There were no sharecropping Jules Verne fans—and not just because he was racist or they couldn't read.

Black geeks are of the "now," in part because they never could have been before. Without the increasing movement of African Americans into the middle class, black geekdom wouldn't even exist. For one, comic books and *Star Trek* DVDs are expensive, but it's not just that. When the Black middle class had a lesser role within African American self-definition, traits of underclass life were misconstrued as elements of Blackness itself. Baggy jeans with one ankle pulled up isn't black; it just means you got your fashion sense from jail. Free cheese wasn't black; it just meant you were broke (but it was delicious—I can't front). It's a dangerous misunderstanding:

If you mistake the traits of poverty for your personal identity, you risk being locked into a position where you're unable to advance without betraying yourself. And that's a dead end. The black-geek aesthetic is a celebration of the freedom from that mind-set, and its cool is doing that in all its nerdy glory.

This is the time of the Geek. As America has moved away from defining itself as an industrial nation, we have increasingly become a country whose greatest export is ideas. Our technological and creative invention is what sets us apart from the rest of the world now. Whereas in the past the richest members of our society have been aristocrats and traditional businessmen, today two of the wealthiest people in the country are huge geeks: Facebook's Mark Zuckerburg and Microsoft's Bill Gates. The impact that has had on the culture has been fast and total. You couldn't make a movie like 1984's *Revenge of the Nerds* in today's world because our perception of geeks has changed so dramatically. The nerds won. The prize wasn't just money; it was social acceptance and even esteem. It was the right to coolness. Those once dismissed as nerdy by society are now seen as its leaders.

It took me years to be as brave as my cousin Alex. To flaunt my inner geek. To reach the self-acceptance necessary to reach cool. Because I wasn't cool with it. I would buy comics, but I would take them from the store in a brown paper bag held close to my stomach sheepishly, as if it were some form of shameful porn. I had an hour bus ride from the shop, but I wouldn't take the comics out until I was safely at home, hidden.

I was fourteen before I went into the store and really looked around at who was next to me. That's when I finally got it. In a neighborhood that was majority white, in that store it was no ethnic cross-section—I was surrounded by other brothers. Blacks and Latinos. Maybe they were just like me, fathers not in the home, searching for the fantasy of power. I don't know. But looking around, I was comfortable. I was at home. I had a people. And they were, for all their acne and dandruff, beautiful.

Coming out to yourself and to others, and then staying out as you walk out the door, brings strength in its action. And then strength in the numbers that join you. The fact that some—regardless of ethnicity—look and scoff at black geeks' bookish airs, that just adds to the coolness of it all. Because a true geek doesn't care. And there is the essence of geek power. It says: *I love something, and I'm going to tell the world I love it, and if you dismiss me for that, it just shows that my love is greater than your scorn. In fact, the more you hate what I love, the more you deride it, the cooler I become. My love is so strong that your disdain means nothing to me. The more you scoff, the stronger I get. I know who I am. I know the beauty I see, and nothing in the world can stop me from singing out that truth with my life. Nothing you can do about it. I like it and I'm not supposed to. I like it, in part, because I'm not supposed to. I have reached coolness by walking in the other direction so far that I went around the world and hit it from the other side.*

CRAZY
RACHEL
M.
HARPER

Growing up, I knew three things for certain about my father: He was brilliant, he was scary, and he was cool. These were not three separate things; they were one thing with three parts, the lines between them almost imperceptible, like the segments of a banana. He was a poet with a facility for language and an incredible memory—the ability to quote Yeats or Du Bois in the middle of an argument, to recite Frost or Auden on the spot, to whistle the entire album of John Coltrane's *A Love Supreme*. He was a large man, well over six feet tall and linebacker solid, but he was light on his feet and strangely graceful for a man of his size. He could walk soundlessly as a cat, appearing to glide across the room, but when he stood still he carried the weight of a mountain in his frame—we knew he could not be moved.

But it was not size alone that made him scary; it was the intensity of his gaze, how he would get quieter the angrier he got, eventually whispering as he delivered the final verdict, doling out the consequence for our crime of breaking the window with a miskicked soccer ball, lighting the quilt on fire, or coming home from the town swimming pool without our little brother. When he was most angry, he wouldn't speak at all, the funk sometimes lasting for days. Somewhere in that space—between the silence, the brooding, and the brilliance—is where he created the cool.

I knew my father was an artist before I knew his birthday or where he was born. It was an obvious part of his identity, like being Black and male, yet forever unspoken. (Like his first name, we never dared use it.) But even without the term, I recognized the behaviors early and came to accept them as part of who he was. They rarely, if ever, got questioned. He spent a month each summer at an artists' colony and most of April (Poetry Month) on the road, giving readings. He typed our birthday cards and gave out couplets as gifts, taught us poems to recite at bedtime instead of prayers. We learned from a young age never to throw away envelopes, since my father often started poems along their edges. A list of words that in other houses would be a grocery list—*milk*, *eggs*, *butter*, *bread*—in our house meant an opening stanza: psalm, syncopate, skeleton, scream.

Even in casual conversation, word choice was everything: not angry, *homicidal*; not happy, *euphoric*. Words seemed to melt in his mouth like ice cubes; something cold and hard, like *exegesis*, softened on his tongue, became fluid like water, and we began to drink it in. He made words a tangible thing,

left margin:

delicate and pretty, like flowers, and suddenly our vocabularies bloomed. In fourth grade I knew the word *opaque*, by sixth grade, *insouciant*.

As children, we learned something else about our father, the artist: not to talk to him while he was working. Which really meant: while he was reading the newspaper, typing a postcard, listening to music, whistling, talking on the phone, flipping through a magazine, staring at a piece of art, rolling quarters, watching highlights from a football game, taking photographs, reading a map, opening mail, or telling a story. All those activities—pretty much everything we saw him do—were, in one form or another, a preamble to the work.

We learned early on that while other fathers went to an office to work, our father went into his mind. Because of this, it appeared to us that he was always working, when in truth, he was more likely thinking about work, dreading work, or dissatisfied with the work he'd already completed. He fought work like a boxer, alternately dancing around the poem with a playful, almost teasing attack, and then beating it down with a series of jabs, a right hook the final blow to finish it off. Part poet, part pugilist. All of this is what made him an artist, but it was also what made him cool.

The instability of his moods made him cool as well: To be unpredictable and unknown in any form is the ultimate embodiment of cool. We did not know how to anticipate his moods or what, exactly, would elicit them, so we were always waiting, expecting them to arrive like a snowstorm. There were common triggers: running late to the airport and rushing onto the crowded plane, the offense of the small seats; a long wait at a restaurant; bad weather; an unexpected phone call; being asked a question he didn't want to answer, one he thought you should already know, or one he was certain he had already answered. The uncommon: an argument with my mother; a car accident; my grandmother's death. His reaction to these events—the shutdown, the silence—was what made him inaccessible to us. He was a tree we could not climb, a land we couldn't conquer.

I don't think it was intentional on his part, that he wanted to be "cool" in our eyes, but it happened nonetheless. It was part of his persona, perhaps created by us as a way to deal with or understand that which we could not understand. We knew he loved us; we knew his periods of silence and the dark moods that accompanied them were not our fault, but were the result of stress, from his students and the politics of academia to the frozen marriage that no amount of sunshine could thaw to the demands of creativity, the result of worshipping at the altar of the muse, whoever or whatever that might have been.

Today he might be called depressed, but that word was never uttered in our house. To us he was moody or in a funk, quiet, withdrawn, even angry—but *not* depressed. To use such a clinical term would have been to look down on him, to judge him, pathologize him, and thus make that part of him somehow strange, foreign, and wrong—make it something that had happened to him, like a sickness or a curse that would then need to be addressed and possibly extracted.

And the notion of that was even scarier than he was. No, we needed him to be cool, because we not only understood cool, but admired it. We could look up to a cool father, even when he ignored us, but not up to a mean or a depressed one.

As we got older, these ideas spread to all the other artists we knew, mostly my father's friends and colleagues. We respected their talents and valued the art that resulted, though we often didn't understand it. Like the artist, the work itself was unknowable to some degree, unachievable by the common man, but the artists had something else in common: They were alike in mood—sullen, temperamental, detached, and passionate. They were what my father often called crazy. Unlike "depressed," "crazy" had cachet, and it was thrown around like a compliment in their circles. To be crazy was to be loved. My father would frequently say, "Man, he was crazy," but what he meant was: *He was brilliant, he was bad, he was beautiful. He was unparalleled; his like will never come again.* My father once said the same phrase standing at the foot of Egypt's Great Pyramid of Giza—"Man, that's crazy"—and I understood that he meant the same thing.

That was the first type of crazy: the state of being brilliant. The second was an event of craziness, when someone just "went crazy." My father would laugh as he told us about a doped-up jazz musician or a drunk poet, stories that always ended with someone in a fight in the alley outside a bar, something scary, violent, and passionate about to occur. He never said it, but we could tell by the sound of his voice, the light in his eye, the sly smile, that it was, in fact, cool to him.

By his account, they were always fighting over the same things—women, drugs, music, and money—but as I got older I began to see that the deeper fight was within each individual. They were fighting not only to assert their identities, but to create them, to solidify and define their myths. They were making the stories of who they were—to themselves, each other, and to the outside world. They were *Black*, which was to be an outsider; they were *artists*, which was to be misunderstood; they were *crazy*, which was to be brilliant, unstable, dangerous. Instead of ruining their reputations, these struggles with addiction—alcohol, drugs, sex, gambling—often heightened their legendary status. But from there the path grew predictable: The craziness increased, the stories grew in number and intensity, the behavior became even more erratic.

Perhaps the link between artist and addict is that both are seekers, looking not only for pathways normally denied, but for avenues that didn't previously exist, that others don't (or can't) even see. Perhaps we share certain personality traits, and, like my father and his friends, a common dark temperament, a touch of supersensitivity, keen perceptions, and boiling passions. As artists, we seem to *desire* like no one else—a desire that often pushes us to the point of madness. We don't just feel a range of intense emotions; we feel the need to express them to others. Express as in expel. Rant. Rage. Purge. Get them out of our heads and bodies and into the world. Onto the paper, the canvas, the keys. *Get it away from us*, we seem to be saying—*this pain, this joy, this madness; take it so we no longer have to carry the burden.* Because we can't carry it alone, and we can't keep it inside.

What a paradox: Kept inside, the pain is poison, but when artists, especially Black artists, let it out, it's genius. But genius is not a typical state with normal expectations; it's acceptable for a genius to act (or actually be) crazy. In fact, we often *want* that in our Black artists. We expect them to be crazy, love them more, in fact—deeper, better—if they are. While we are afraid of the darkness that the artist appears to create from, but we love the creation. It is a mystery to us. And when we are solving a mystery, the answer—sometimes obvious, sometimes inconceivable—is often not as interesting once we understand it. We don't want to understand them, to see them, because to be unseen is to be unknown, and mystery is the birth of cool. So we give a wide berth around Black artists' mystery, granting them space and air. We don't want to undercover their secrets fully, to see the faces beneath the masks.

And so we romanticize the black or blue moods until the genius withdraws into the cave and we don't hear from him or her for years; then we get restless and begin to lose faith. We are always open to the return, of course, but we fear, in the meantime, that they have been eaten by the bear that also hibernates in that cave. When they don't return, when they trade in their art for drugs, addiction, suicide, we are often devastated, but not surprised. How long can a person live in a cave without becoming a bear?

Black blues has become more than a myth in our culture, it's become a product, another commodity we package and sell to the mainstream to show who we are, with the intention not of being better understood, but of becoming human in the eyes of white America. We suffer, we bleed, we cry—therefore we are. Every American may not understand the need to do this, but the legacy of African Americans in this country (yes, I'm talking about slavery) is to always have the existence of our psyches in question. As Black people we wear masks, some that say, *I'm okay, I'm normal, I'm nonthreatening,* and others that say, *I'm strong, I'm invincible, I'm cool.* We hide in plain sight.

We may choose to wear masks, but the power of our very presence in contemporary American society gives us the opportunity to show a wide range of emotional expressions. Surpassing all other labels, Black artists are human beings—living, breathing, passionate souls. Cool has never meant cold. We respond to loss and devastation with the same fervor as anyone else, and so there is no disputing our humanity. But, being artists, we take it one step further: We turn our loss, our heartache, into art—we give it life. So it then exists beyond our own bodies (our own selves), becoming timeless and universal. That transformation, that artistic creation, is the ultimate form of power—the ability to take something intangible and make it real. What, in the end, is more cool than that?

Clinical depression, a psychological state that requires diagnosis and treatment, is quite different from a funk an artist intentionally falls into, hoping to access a well of creativity

previously unavailable. But for some, the two terms are invariably linked. Was my father depressed during my childhood? Perhaps. Would medication and therapy have helped? Probably. Would they have affected his creativity? Possibly. But that was a gamble he was unwilling to take. And I can't say I blame him.

Sure, it would have been nice for him to smile more and brood less, but not at the expense of his art. If the upsets in his life (the losses, the heartaches) led to the creation of beautiful poems, who am I to say that wasn't a worthwhile trade? The legacy in the library is what remains, which today seems as important as the stories my brothers and I also carry. In enjoying his poetry—like we enjoy Morrison's prose, Baldwin's essays, Coltrane's riffs, Pryor's jokes, or Basquiat's art—we are enjoying a piece of his pain as well: the artistry that was born of that pain. We look at those artists as we look upon our mothers during childbirth: We don't want them to suffer in order to bring us into the world, but we are damn happy to be alive.

I once asked my father why he became a poet. "I had no choice," he said. "Poetry chooses you." Perhaps the only choice the artist has is whether to accept the gift as a blessing or a curse. My father seemed to think it was both, and he accepted all the associations—from crazy to cool—that came with it. Though it may have compromised some of his most intimate relationships, it did not compromise his most fundamental creed: that above all else, the art must survive.

RESERVE
HELENA
ANDREWS

When I was thirteen, I came home to nobody. My mother was gone. There wasn't a note. This wasn't unusual. After sitting on the couch totally unfazed for more than an hour, watching afternoon reruns, I was surprised by a knock. "Your mother's in jail," my grandmother said from the other side of the screen door, her face shaded by the dark netting. Mesh or no mesh, I wouldn't have been able to read her. Her face was always inscrutable. "You're gonna stay over at my house for a while," she said, opening the door without invitation and walking into the living room. Waiting.

I didn't miss my cue. I got up, headed silently to my room, packed my school uniform and underwear, and stomped my way to Grandmommy's smoke-filled '92 Nissan. We rode the entire way without words. Frances, my mother, called later—"Lena Dana, don't worry about it, baby. You're strong. You can handle this." I answered with a few muttered "mmmkays," because I knew I had no choice in the matter.

I hung up, studied for AP English, sat on the MTA for an extra hour each way to school, and waited for my mother to come home.

The point: My face never changed. I was immutable. To get by without her, I had to be. My mask saved me, cloaking whatever was going on underneath with an autopilot *I'm okay* that spoke volumes. It brought me from my grandmother's shotgun house on 108th and Vermont all the way downtown to my spotless private school at Fourth and Commonwealth. That was the first time I put on that mask and it felt good. I was cool. I had to be—to keep from falling apart.

There's something curious that happens to Black girls on their way to puberty: We disappear into an imaginary telephone booth and emerge as miniature superheroes. Hit by a speeding bullet of outside forces—race-based sexism and society's impossible expectations—former civilians begin to take cover behind an ancient mask of impenetrability. Our secret identity—sweet, innocent, approachable—becomes just that, a secret. It's the identity we share with only a trusted few, the small circle we've vetted and deemed worthy.

In Toni Morrison's *The Bluest Eye*, a little girl named Claudia says, "We had become headstrong, devious, and arrogant. Nobody paid us any attention, so we paid very good attention to ourselves. Our limitations were not known to us— then." That story, set in the 1940s, could tell every Black girl's story since slavery. Generations of Black women have grown up outside the spotlight, becoming "headstrong, devious, and arrogant" because nobody has paid them any attention. They have become wildly successful self-soothers—tending to themselves by cutting off the outside with a restraint that serves as mask, shield, and safe house.

When it comes to the world at large, they're too far gone to be their regular selves, for fear of disappointing the faceless masses they've been sworn to protect. In Zora Neale Hurston's seminal novel, *Their Eyes Were Watching God*, Janie's grandmother explains the plight of the early-twentieth-century Black woman this way: "De nigger woman is de mule uh de world so far as Ah can see."

One hundred years later, many Black women still see their role in society as having to carry the weight of the world on their backs, like an army of Atlases. So these little women become warriors in a fight they didn't start. A fight that began before they were born with the side-eye, the B-girl stance, the nonviolent resistance of the Civil Rights movement, and the denial of emotion during slavery. Their weapon of choice throughout the centuries? Stoic reserve.

It's an ancient artifact passed down from generation to generation of Black women. To be clear, no one's ever actually held it, but we all know it when we see it and we put it on when we need it to become powerful. A rite of passage disguised as a hand-me-down, our mask is tangible but untouchable, worn down from years of good use. It's the steely look of detachment the outside world gets when they call to us from the corner ("Hey shawtay") or in the club

("Excuse me, miss") or into an office ("Hey, can you pop in for a sec?").

Silently, the mask can speak volumes. It can say, *Don't talk to me, touch me, or trap me.* It can say, *I have power over every situation,* even when she so clearly does not. This is our coolness coat of arms, our impenetrable shield. What some might call the bitch face, I call the survival side-eye.

Consider this familiar scene: It's morning rush hour in Anywhere Urban, USA. Slicing through the sidewalk traffic jam of bodies attached to BlackBerrys, corner-to-corner salesmen, and their clientele scrabbling toward the metro, is the successful Black woman. She stands out. She is something different—from the way she carries herself to the look on her face. Cars honk as she crosses the street, accepting only slightly their presence in *her* universe. She grabs a free newspaper from a man handing them out near the station's entrance and ignores the catcalls begging her to "smile more."

She disappears down the escalator, staring straight ahead like a woman on a mission. She swipes her card and glides through the automatic turnstile without pause. The blinking red lights on the platform's edge indicate a train is coming soon. The train's door stops directly in front of where she's standing, as if arriving solely for her benefit. When it opens, she steps through and unfolds the newspaper under her arm at the same time. As if choreographed, her movements seem both deliberate and totally spontaneous. She seems to be doing more than everyone else by doing so much less. Your eye is drawn to her. She acknowledges your presence by ignoring it. She is the personification of cool by annihilating your very existence.

Black women perform this ritual instinctually, so used to the consistent soundtrack of white noise that surrounds us. The distance we keep from the rest of the world is not just an urban habit, it's genetically etched in the wooden lines of our faces. With just one look, Black women keep a cool distance between ourselves and reality rushing toward us on a daily basis and achieve the superhuman ability to live above our world—making living in it possible. What the unwitting public doesn't know about the mask is that there is more than just practiced bravado behind that invisible shield. There is an innate survival skill that allows Black women to move stealthily and safely from street corner to corner office.

I've always considered myself an overachiever with underachiever expectations. As a kid I was clinically superstitious, holding my breath until I got picked next to last for kickball and murdering flowers until their petals told me what I wanted to hear. My quiet rituals were unknown to all but me. And they usually worked. I figured good things happen to those who play it cool. When you assume everything will work in your favor, things usually do. Hopped up on ramen noodles, I hurdled from intern to temp to grad student to staff writer by pretending not to care whether I fell. The mask I wore said, *I got this*, while my inner dialogue was something more along the lines of, *Oh shit oh shit oh shit.*

Among Yoruba women there is a mask called the *oloju foforo*, which means "the owner of the deep-set eyes." The name refers to the squarelike holes cut into the mask's surface, just beneath the painted eyes. The holes enable the wearer to actually see out from behind. It's as if the woman wearing the *oloju foforo* has two sets of eyes: the one the world sees, which stays immutable and wooden, and the one that the wearer uses to see the world. Other parts of the mask mark a Yoruba woman's spiritual self, or "inner head." There's a clear distinction between her inner and outer identities—the former is celebrated, and it is hidden from view, protected, perhaps, by the latter.

All this made sense to me when I met a writer I admired in the cafeteria at the *New York Times*' headquarters in Manhattan. I'd never seen her in person but was positive, based on her use of colloquialisms in the country's most revered newspaper, that she was cool by default. I had to know her. Her monotone never rose higher than *I'm so over it*, whether she was talking about planning her wedding or interviewing pop stars. We talked about how I was so over being professional while Black. How I constantly felt as if I had to circumscribe the stereotypes of my race within the confines of my job description, making sure to use my "white-people voice," smaller than my real one. All I really did was answer phones and find plastic forks, but still, it seemed as if people were too frightened to even attempt to relate to me—"I mean, it's not like I was banging on African drums all weekend. You *can* ask how it went."

She laughed and then leaned in, as if to tell me a secret. "Everybody here knows me," she said. "I don't know them, but they know who I am. You can always use that to your advantage." Her reputation would always precede her, and because she was a Black woman who wore the mask, it always would. She couldn't get away from it, so instead of trying to, she used it as an entrée.

One of the few reporters at the *New York Times* who knew my name, Warren Leary, gave me this advice: "Kid, you always gotta look two jobs ahead." That's part of Black cool—always looking ahead, up and over, but never really at something. So I ignored my job title, news assistant, and started writing stories like a reporter. Then I became a reporter, who in the end couldn't actually stand reporting. "I hate everybody" became my new "good morning." I used the mask I wore to my new job every day as a means to get through it.

It hid the look of disappointment on my face when an editor asked me some detail about Michelle Obama's mannerisms or background, always couching the question first with, "Okay, I'm not asking you this because you're the only Black woman in the room, but . . . " The mask also made me, at twenty-five, look like an expert on everything. The uniformity, the nonchalance, and the distance spoke for me, opening up opportunities I'd never have had without it—heading to North Carolina to cover the 2008 presidential elections, telling a million viewers on CNN what "people" thought about the Obamas. Eventually though, unwavering expertise would pull me down into a typhoon of too-much-ness—too much work, too much pressure, too much stress. I was taking a mental-health day when I got the call that someone else's mask had broken.

One of my best friends from college wore her mask along with the rest of us. Back then it wasn't much—maybe just a blank stare and a brisk walk through the quad. But she was one of the innocents, someone who wore the mask just barely, briefly. We made fun of her for that—the regular joke was that she was "such a nerd before we made her cool." But secretly we envied her restraint. She could survive with the side-eye.

Then we graduated, got jobs, and kept it moving from bullet point to bullet point as our Black-girl GPS's directed us, zombielike, through the next decade. We started to notice that she even wore the mask among friends, her cool turning into a frigidity that became a front. So we, the people who supposedly knew her best, figured that, like us, she was doing just fine. That she was "successful." Until we got the call that she had been tired, that she had been lonely, and that she had quit us, this, life.

Sometimes the mask takes over. Instead of allowing a Black woman ease of access by making her untouchable, it can limit her by making her invisible, one-dimensional. Instead of saving its wearer, it can suffocate her.

The value of the mask as a costume quick change is easy to recognize. Ignoring the invention of the perm, Black chicks are rarely, if ever, susceptible to magic. We don't go up in pillars of smoke. We don't disappear down suspect rabbit holes. And we don't walk into coat closets, never to be heard from again. But somewhere along the journey from slave to soul sister to single lady, we did learn how to shape-shift. We learned how to make our own magic, and it all started with an ancient face—lips pursed, cheeks flattened, eyes straight ahead. Who wouldn't want to be at once strong and Black? But the mask can be both a necessary tool in our arsenal and a gun to our "inner heads."

My grandmother taught me that the week I was trapped at her house. The week my mother was in a jail cell and I felt imprisoned in the guest room of a woman I barely knew. I knew what my grandmother looked like, sure, but I'd never really *seen* her. My strategy was to stay out of her way by constantly looking busy. If she could do it, so could I. But I slipped one night as I put the finishing touches on some homework. Bored, I glanced up from my books and stared at my grandmother's face for what couldn't have been more than five seconds. Sensing my gaze, she whipped around with a metal spoon in her hand. "What are you staring at?" she barked. "I'm doing what I'm supposed to be doing in here. You do what you're supposed to be doing in there." With that, she swiveled back around, making me dinner because my mother couldn't.

Back then, thirteen-year-old me didn't get it. Why couldn't I have just stared at her? Perhaps it was because she didn't want me to see the fact that she was tired. She was sixtysomething, still cleaning up her fortysomething retired hippie daughter's messes. After all those years, she still had to wear the mask that had gotten her through the great migration, a war of a marriage, eight children, and as many jobs. She'd had her mask on for so long, it was part of her skin. My grandmother had shade built in—she didn't need Anna Wintour's sunglasses. I admired it. I was afraid of it. And eventually I borrowed it.

But my cool comes and goes. I can control it now. I know when my mask gives me superpowers and also when it can be my Kryptonite. I can be strong and Black and reserved when masking my "inner head" protects my secret identity. The trick is to know when to take it off before it takes over.

THE HIPSTER
DAYO
OLOPADE

Mali in the 1960s was a hip place. It should not have been so: Bamako, the capital, anchors a landlocked wedge of West African desert and grass. Yet the country's unusually young, urban population spent the first decade of Mali's freedom from French colonial rule smoking Marlboros and drinking locally brewed Castle lagers, doing the eyebrow-raising things that hipsters do. A decade later, a dysfunctional, militarized government would force a sudden good-bye to all that, but for the boom years, Bamako boomed, and a young photographer named Malick Sidibé took its pulse.

Sidibé's open-air works freeze Black bodies on white nights, dancing, clapping, sweating, and chasing smoke rings in flight. His studio portraiture distills this exuberance into pure pulp. In one photo, *Fou de Disque*, a young man vamps in profile, his face hidden by the lapel of his period-perfect trench coat. His Afro is lean, but a halo of vinyl records pasted on the wall behind him recalls a Medusan tousle of hair. Another black-and-white, *Yeye,* depicts a teen with an impossibly slim waist easing into a pose that the differently proportioned Fat Joe would popularize with the 2004 single "Lean Back." In Malian *bogolan* prints, Elton John sunglasses, and fey disco pants, the kids are cool without dispute. Their outfits are just outfits. The fun is really fun.

Contrast the purity of the Malians' self-regard with the tortured and performative notions of the hipster in contemporary America. The traits are as obvious as a neck tattoo: Hipsters are urban, privileged, attitudinally earnest, and functionally alternative. They live life at the intersection of Pabst Blue Ribbon and Day-Glo leggings—worn with irony, or maybe not. The prototype listens to indie darlings like Pavement, or anthem rock like Arcade Fire. Maybe even a little Wu-Tang. Everything obscure is good: homemade pickles, a headband on some longhair of a man, a waifish girl sporting several thick gold chains. And, for the most part, the hipster is white.

Of course, the origins of the word, as Mark Greif takes care to point out in the collection of essays on hipsterism produced by *n+1* magazine, are Black. Norman Mailer parsed "The White Negro" in a 1954 issue of *Dissent* magazine:

> *Indeed if one is to be a man, almost any kind of unconventional action often takes disproportionate courage. So it is no accident that the source of Hip is the Negro for he has been living on the margin between totalitarianism and democracy for two centuries.*

James Baldwin famously scolded Mailer for his fetishization of Black cool. But, in a sense, Mailer was right: The hipster will always be defined in opposition to majority culture. For the white hipster—torn between ironic, "who cares if I'm wearing a tracksuit" detachment and the exhibitionism required to perform the trend—such opposition requires effort. The explosive outer edges of American punk culture today have been colonized by Mexicans, some of whose very presence in the United States is transgressive. By contrast, white, urban twentysomethings bought (into) the physical trappings of hipsterism out of necessity. It's the curse, perhaps, of majority culture. Lacking both social outsidership and whatever traces of melanin that would brand one as truly outré, young white Americans are forced to perform any distinctions with aggressively curated eclecticism. John Leland calls this "Caucasian kitsch."

This explains the iterations of white hipsterism in the 1990s and 2000s: bike-breaking mechanical collectives in Austin, Texas; Dumpster-diving vegan brunches in Brooklyn, New York; alternative-rock bands from Baltimore, Maryland, who perform in animal attire. According to Greif, the burgeoning, irony-obsessed white subculture donned trucker hats yet shunned SUVs, and wore pants tight enough to cloud traditional ideas of identity and sexuality. Even the protesters who flooded the Seattle G8 summit with crocodile tears began to register their distaste at the level of consumption. As the George W. Bush years wore on, this physically manifested political difference was the point.

As hipsterism migrated from Black to white, it likewise evolved from a state of cool to something you can buy. Describing the relentless march of gentrification in the Lower East Side of Manhattan, Greif takes pains to point this out: "If the hipster then spent $1,000 on clothes, or a painted skateboard, or Johnnie Walker Blue Label—it seemed like rebellion." White-hipster disillusion thrives in equal measure on church-sale vintage T-shirts and on apps downloaded to Apple's iPhone. As a result, today's hipster is splashier and less Western. Kids in Croatia and Dubai wear bright sneakers and graphic hoodies that they have purchased in stores promising that version of the American dream. Pure consumption offers entry into what has drifted from Black cool to white hype.

In a strange convergence during the same swath of the late nineties and early '00s, Black style also became about performative consumption. In 1999—the same year as the anti-G8 "Battle in Seattle"—Hype Williams filmed a portrait of the Magnolia Housing Projects in New Orleans. It was a music video for Juvenile's hit song "Ha." There's a gritty charm to the dancing, as joyful as 1960s Mali. As the pseudo-documentary footage suggests, the grind is real—but bling is king. About three minutes into the video, you can see a child version of rapper Lil Wayne, who grew up at Magnolia. He, like the star of the video, is gleefully waggling a golden chain.

This iteration of Black American cool offered a type of social solidarity (who doesn't remember sweating FUBU's apparel and Blackronym, "for us by us"?). But for the most part, fashion choices reflected an ethics of consumption geared not at opposition but at mainstreaming—melding Black difference with majority mores (Tommy Hilfiger in size XXL, please). Though hipsterism is the heritage of Black American cities, the generation reared on Nautica and K-Swiss forged an association with whiteness that left Black hipsters on the outskirts of Black cool. In the 2009 film *Medicine for Melancholy*, two such characters amble around the bleachening city of San Francisco. One principal, Micah (played by *Daily Show* correspondent Wyatt Cenac), laments, "Everything about being indie is tied to not being Black."

Micah means that the trappings of "Caucasian kitsch" that populate his everyday require mental dissociation from Blackness. For the racially alternative hipster, any act of self-expression is necessarily hurling itself against an entrenched, if recent, narrative about what it is to be Black.

I have always considered myself a hipster, or one for as long as I've known the term. I'm a Nigerian American cosmopolite with a soft spot for LCD Soundsystem and vintage boots. I was the first and only Black editor in chief of the *Yale Literary Magazine*, the sort of game that feeds the sort of game that is *n+1*. For four birthdays running I served up PBR *and* jerk chicken, to all comers. I enjoy Wu-Tang tracks but feel greater affection for the seventies soul samples that scaffold their best work. Is this lonely? Perhaps.

But I'd argue that the in-between-ness and subversion Micah bemoans are actually an asset. Today's Black cool is a smart-alecky evolution of the carelessness in 1960s Mali. In

September 2011, the *New York Times* published a thorough examination of evolving Black style, anchored by two young men with a passion for refined streetwear (think tweed, and pocket squares made from kente cloth). "I used to wear size 42 jeans," one modern dandy told the reporter. "Coming from that to a tie and shirt, people perceive you in a whole different way."

The surprise is the point. Their blog, Street Etiquette, doesn't wholly abandon the brands of nineties Black style. The hood-zuberance of "Ha" remains—but the Polo sweaters fit. This version of Black cool is defined by fusion, hacking, and recycling—especially white revisions of an originally Black attitude. Ask Andre 3000 in pearls: It is a performance of a performance.

Who knows this best? The kids in cities from Detroit to Dallas to Washington, D.C., mixing white-boy silhouettes, postpunk swagger, and Elvis Costello eyeglass frames. Take the young Black men who comprise the New Boyz—a California band that has recorded a series of YouTube videos designed to teach their signature dance—the "jerk." The boys are wearing electric-colored T-shirts and pin-thin trousers in contrasting neon hues. One is wearing several silver necklaces and a fedora. The knee-popping, stylized locking that characterizes "jerking" has spread from coast to coast—junior high school students in New York City have picked up on the lo-fi West Coast rhythms of the New Boyz. Responding to concerns that "jerking" came from "gang" culture, a precocious ten-year-old told a reporter, "We changed it and made it something positive and new. We made it ours."

This child represents what I'll call the "kick, push" generation—obsessed with skateboarding, sure, but also with the radical re-curation and re-creation of diverse foundational myths and touchstones. In Washington, D.C., where I lived for years, you can see Black kids skating alongside white kids, whom they outnumber, despite living in a city where the Black population has declined from three-fourths to just over half. The real question, then: Who is gentrifying whom?

Let's return to Sidibé. We start with the external. The fashions are visible. There is something in the glass, something on the radio. Yet the subjects of his work suggest that it does not matter what is in the glass, or who is on the radio. The subversion is immaterial. These Africans are not warring and dying and emigrating. They're dancing. Their hipsterism is, finally, about attitude, born of an understanding that they are spectacular. In one of Sidibé's later photographs, of teenagers peering out from a lake, the youths are wearing nothing at all—only the look of restrained amusement reserved for those they are used to catching watching.

THE BREAK
VALORIE
THOMAS

I gotta, gotta keep my balance
High or low
Whether you're high or low
You gotta tip on the tightrope
—Janelle Monae

As Fu-Kiau Bunseki remarked to me, "Every time there
is a break in a pattern, that is the rebirth of [ancestral]
power in you."
—Robert Farris Thompson

The women in my family never met a riff they didn't like. Even their names are stories improvised from experience: Olive aka Wuful; Mavis; Jaye; and Olive aka Big Olive aka Munner aka O.G. (yes). They would sit in the kitchen talking through the night about everything from relationships to revolution to who Robert Johnson met at the crossroads to Mahalia Jackson singing "The Upper Room" to Johnny

Mathis's and Grace Jones's performances of gender and race. The concept of the break and the accompanying shimmering vertigo of falling into the crossroads where the freedom of invention cuts in resonates with me, because I was raised by four women who lived their entire lives immersed in Black vernacular, respecting it as an inexhaustible source of spontaneity, irony, intellectual insight, and joy.

The break, that point where a song stops for a drum or other instrumental interlude or improv, is a trademark of African diaspora music. The break adds a new element that challenges the structure of a composition, as in the original contemporary crossover example of James Brown's "Cold Sweat": "Give the drummer some! . . . Give the bass player some!" This is where assumptions are overturned and narrative arcs change. Grey Gundaker points out in *Signs of Diaspora, Diaspora of Signs* that African break patterning activates double voicing, double vision, and cross-rhythms that challenge the status quo, "challenging seemingly fixed relations between top and bottom, high and low, foreground and background, and the framing of events themselves . . . It also amounts to the claim that real mastery . . . means knowledge and movement in all directions—down, around, under, and through, not just up and over, not merely in the ruler lines of alphabetic text." The break, whether in music or other forms, sets a condition of vertigo in motion that tests mastery and movement in all directions at once.

From an African or neo-African perspective, exercising grace and skill under the intense pressure of being in vertigo—

whirling, spinning, falling at the same time, in chaotic un-differentiated space—is the product of *iwa rere*, ethical be-havior, and *iwa pele*, compassion. In *Flash of the Spirit*, Robert Farris Thompson notes that such graceful skill can restore the balance that is *itutu*, the power of mystic coolness, the balance of reason, sanity, and gentle character that provides "critical focus" for human action. Thompson remarks that through *itutu*, "we find the confidence to cope with all kinds of situations. This is *áshe*. This is character. This is mystic coolness. All one." The break is always an opportunity to demonstrate *itutu*.

James Brown said "make it funky," and his use of the break gave birth to funk and hip-hop, genres that along with electronica at their core support progressive social change by inspiring what critically acclaimed DJ, producer, and cultural activist Garth Trinidad identifies as "thought that drove dialogue among youth . . . a powerful tool that could incite emotion, desire, and intelligent thought about current events." After he introduced artists such as Meshell Nde-geocello, Jill Scott, Les Nubians, Floetry, Kelis, M.I.A., Van Hunt, Gnarls Barkley, King Britt, Res, Sa-Ra, and J*DaVeY to the mainstream, the program format of Trinidad's long-running L.A. radio show, *Chocolate City* (KCRW), motivated the Grammy Awards' introduction of the Urban/Alterna-tive category in 2003.

In response to people who ask for "something I can dance to" on the basis of a limited musical range shaped by mainstream airwaves, Trinidad "would love to press pause in a moment and take them into a parallel universe and teach them about why they need me to play something faster so that they can feel more comfortable . . . The experience can be stressful, annoying and wonderful." Trinidad's video self-portrait, *Sound and Vision Intro*, depicts a diasporic subject who is completely still, alert, and calm, coolly stationed in the urban vertigo of a fragmented landscape. Dark glasses signifying double vision, he engages the viewer from shifting locations marked by broken lines, angles, ragged thresholds, speeding bodies and vehicles, and voids.

In a 2007 blog post titled "Anatomy of a Zombie," Trinidad situates the DJ's role as cultural worker in an ethics of break culture, theorizing "a responsibility to break new ideas and push music forward without alienating the audience . . . to generate balance." That the break has been electronically altered, digitized, and amped into the sample and compound editing of the cut attests to the survival of a sense of democratic agency in hip-hop that affirms artistic innovation and a radical social critique.

The break in African diaspora music and cultural expression is a transformative technology that mirrors the vitality, dissonances, and underlying coherence of diasporic cultural processes. As a metaphor—and in performance, insofar as it represents a step out of the familiar structure of a song or dance into another consciousness that is different from but still part of the narrative arc—the break is a kind of possession that intervenes on, but does not invalidate, the communal links on which it depends. The break, the crossroads, and the void signify the potency that haunts the space between forms (as hidden genealogy). Vertigo is a signal aspect of the literacy of *itutu*, an epistemology of undifferentiated space that holds strategies for negotiating cultural trauma, disruption, dislocation, and hybridity in pointed resistance to colonial erasure. Everything is possible in the break.

That is the space of cultural resistance in which slaves are able to imagine freedom from dominance. The dominant consciousness has always produced a monologue dedicated to serving white male privilege and property. Double consciousness, W. E. B. Du Bois's theory that Black subjectivity is always watching itself move through a society constructed by racism, asserts a break or fracturing of that monologue that makes other kinds of movement, and decolonized subjectivities, possible. A collaboratively constructed, critically informed vernacular social reality is the invisible ground on which double consciousness floats, so to speak, as a healthy response to the annihilating impulse of racism. Because the dominant culture is still organized on the assumption that the mental constructs of colonized and indigenous people lack theoretical and critical value, the "native" is still a Caliban in the dominant view, assigned the task of embodying limitation and the past. The critical substance of indigenous systems of thought has scarcely been regarded as knowledge, though collected and catalogued as artifact. It's time this changed, and, to paraphrase Nigerian musician and composer Fela Kuti, music is one of the weapons; understanding the poetics and politics of the break is another.

Here's a story: My great-grandmother, Munner/O.G., had nine brothers and sisters. They lived in Georgia. Her mother was Black, Indian, and white, and her father was Haitian. When they went to the movies, O.G. and her darker-skinned sister, Lena, sat in the Colored section while their siblings passed to get White Only seats. When the brothers and sisters started passing full-time, O.G., Lena, and a younger brother, Kenny, left for Missouri, stayed Black, and, as far as I know, never spoke to the rest again.

In recalling this story, I focus on epistemic rupture: fragmentation (of family, of self), transgression (of racial lines), improvisation, and insistence on surviving as Black people in a society bent on erasing all signs of Black self-worth (especially the vernacular Blackness associated with being dark, poor, and from the ghetto or "country"). Freefall became the path to reinvention and healing. As a matter of fact, my family never ran into an epistemic break they couldn't handle; vernacular sensibility and double consciousness saw them through many a crossroads moment, with the view that you could live to laugh about it and, by the way, work the crisis in to make a way out of no way.

The soundtrack of my family's world was "Ain't Nobody's Business If I Do"; they listened to red, gold, and black 33s and 78s by Etta, Dinah, Esther, Nancy, Shirley, Carmen, Billy, Lionel, and the Count. They had 1920s black-and-white photos of themselves in beaded headbands and sequined gypsy skirts, playing ukuleles and clarinets, standing on flatbeds pulled by mules, and pictures of their grandmothers standing by fences with shotguns. They had other pictures of themselves standing next to Satchmo by the railroad tracks, and in the chorus line at the Regal Theater. In my mother's lifetime, Aretha, James, Prince, and Chaka were added to the playlist. Outsiders might describe my family as survivors; but *survivor* doesn't begin to convey who these people were in the world.

They were consummate practitioners of their own Black female vernacular ways of reading, and nothing was beyond interpretation. This practice reflected their values, spiritual orientation, and aesthetic. Certainly flawed, they nonetheless defined themselves by aspiring to love and civility instead of hate. In a racist world, they refused to practice racism, while at the same time confronting the realities of race. Though often disappointed by men, they refused to scapegoat anyone. While tipping on the tightrope of poverty, they never considered themselves poor, or anyone's inferior.

They were downright ecstatic about the possibility of never being trapped by someone else's rigid definition of their abilities. These women saw no reason to apologize for themselves, and if other people couldn't deal with them, they didn't mind that, either. They taught me, by example, about being shape-shifting Black women, human beings capable of maintaining the narrative of themselves with integrity and coherence while traveling multiple paths through multiple personas, roles, and circumstances.

This began my education in vertigo: standing by Louis Armstrong on the train tracks, making music on mule-drawn wagons, whispering with your mother's ghost in the middle of the night. They sang to me in French and Japanese and taught me the perfect *jêté*, the steps and words to "Ballin' the Jack," and the meaning of "Flat Foot Floogie (with a Floy Floy." They made us know about having African and Native American roots, why white America tried to distort and destroy those memories, and the importance of recalling and honoring all our ancestors.

My great-aunt taught me multiplication and poetry in a house full of women who called each other "witchy" because they predicted babies, made ringworm disappear by soaking a copper penny in vinegar to place on the afflicted cheek, picked up the phone before it rang, called wild birds to feed from their palms, and routinely conjured their desires through intention and prayer. They had no fear of the unexpected, and so were irreverent, eccentric, artistic, self-invented, contrary, and subject to show up, or leave, in the middle of the night. When the rug was pulled from under, they were still *on it*, diving into freefall until they came up with something new or old or both, and workable. They could do this because they had their own spin; they held an intention to stay resilient and keep valuing one another *na matta what*. They were women defined by movement and resistance, and while they could function well enough in one place, they taught me to resist ever being put in my place or held captive by someone else's plans.

My mother's scene was Esther Phillips "Live at the Parisian Room," hanging with Chi-town friends from our old neighborhood on Budlong, or walking the shoreline at Venice Beach after midnight. She was an artist whose passion was sidelined by administrative work in a government office and by being a divorced single parent to three kids. We often moved with the flow of money.

Some of my childhood was accordingly spent in that part of South-Central L.A. known as The Jungle—acres on acres of 1960s-era tropical and glittering space age–themed apartments turned ghetto, as if Robert Goulet and the Jetsons had premonitions of poverty and Black people and forgot to move in. The streets are lined with palm trees, but everybody knows this place is called The Jungle because the police and the white parts of the city believe this zone is inhabited by savages. It's an urban reservation, a funkified break in the Botoxed facade of La-La Land, where the walls are the whispering tires of police cruisers. The flat-roofed apartment buildings of The Jungle are painted with large identifying numbers for the convenience of patrolling police helicopters known as "ghetto birds."

Those times when my mother spirited us out of an apartment in the middle of the night because she couldn't afford rent that month even while working full-time, we always had a place with family. This movement was turbulent, but the women in my family were people prepared for any and every eventuality, who reserved the right . . . the right to say yes to their own imaginings, the right to say no, the right to change directions or leave in the middle—of plans, of allegiances to men, of sentences.

My family's ability to navigate existential freefall, a condition I now recognize as cultural and personal vertigo, amounts to an ethos and critical strategy inspired by a vernacular lens on the world. Blending wit, irony, and double consciousness to navigate shifting and change is in fact a stabilizing methodology. Vernacular suppleness produces an inner stability that exists independent of external circumstance. That suppleness was constituted by a collectivist, improvisational relationship to language in all its guises—not just written and spoken, but extended even to the visual and visceral. They read their world with an agency supported by collective vernacular logic. It fortified their resistance to the pathological chaos of racism, sexism, and class warfare that constantly threatened to intern their desires and horizons. They revered knowledge and practicality, and the imaginative landscape they constructed was an endlessly fascinating mundane world whose foundation was firmly anchored in their awareness of spirit. They knew without doubt that everything had a spiritual component, and they found this fact hilariously entertaining and gravely important.

I am unapologetically vernacular, and my upbringing was an education in learning to manage epistemic rupture, rather than fear it; the break inspires possibilities and improvisations. I didn't think of it as being raised "in vertigo" at the time—that language came later—but the condition was one of turning, shifting, and constantly changing, nonetheless. For my family, the vernacular was/is not an exotic oddity, a marginal condition, simple entertainment, or a source of shame;

it is an ethos, a locus of consciousness, a stabilizing force, and a critical method rooted in the collective memory that coolness of the soul comes from balanced compassion, will, and wit. Their vernacular worldview did not, as they saw it, conflict with aspirations to education, careers, or social freedom. Vernacular wisdom informed their ethical views, sense of community, and democratic values. My family's acclimation to vertigo kept me from fearing the abrupt motion that life sometimes was, and sometimes called into play.

When my mother died suddenly of heart failure at the age of fifty-nine, I was jolted sideways, through imperceptible holes in a suddenly fluid material world. No perception was accurate, because the constant was random, unpredictable change. Life became a roller coaster of panic attacks and spatial disorientation, and the one word that described it all was inescapable: *vertigo*.

I healed by placing my sense of being in a personal diaspora in relationship to the collective African diaspora, and the diasporas of Native Americans and other indigenous people. There are collective subjectivities and individual imaginative landscapes at stake in the formation of diasporas. Diaspora shapes the body that finds itself, or faces the task of finding itself, in sudden, traumatic motion (think Transatlantic Slave Trade, Middle Passage, colonialism, genocide, refugees). The motion intrinsic to diaspora means that imaginative horizons are perpetually shifting, that the subjective, conceptual aspects of diaspora are as significant as geographies and material practices. Psychological landscapes of diasporas are all borderland, composed of thresholds upon thresholds; in the landscape of shifting borders, centers are ephemeral, not meant to hold because they are illusions in the first place.

As citizens of diaspora, we live in vertigo, and it is our vernacular knowledge that provides *itutu*, cool: the metaphors, language, and practices that reclaim, remix, and decolonize this break we call home.

RESISTANCE
MICHAELA
angela
DAVIS

To the white, privileged, the well-intentioned liberals who have studied us, slept with us, and sympathized with our struggle, and to the with-it pop academics who lived in the hood or built houses in Haiti because you know us, love us, worked and fought on our behalf, know this: All that affords you no rights and no access to this. I deeply appreciate your sympathetic, possessive, or loving service, but you cannot have this. Nope, not this, not now, not ever.

You cannot have our cool-ass Black style.

You cannot determine its existence. You cannot define it. You cannot be the primary source of the validation of its creation, nor give the expert explanation to penetrate the collective cultural imagination. You can't have credit for discovering its brilliance, because if you do, it ain't cool no more, ya dig? White cold examination kills Black cool. So step the fuck back, okay, baby?

This ain't gonna be one of those feel-good odes, like, ooh, look how we tip our hat just like that, or Miles Davis and Jimi Hendrix had mystical style that could blow your mind, or how about that Grace Jones—wasn't she something? Grace freaked Jean-Paul Goude all the way out and left Paris burning. And let us not forget the original Parisian Star Child, Madame Josephine, who danced with Hemingway dressed only in a men's camel coat, her dangerously gorgeous Black body naked underneath, electrifying the lining, his crotch, and any fruit-filled getup her bewitching flesh touched. And let us not forget our soul style on celluloid, *Shaft* and *Get Christy Love*—weren't they just *Super Fly*?

I will not write, at least not right now, another celebration song of our swag, our genius way of taking something from nothing and changing whole industries. I'm not going to proclaim how "Black folks activate clothes" or something like, "Black people don't wear fashion, they perform it."

This will not be one of those precious but pitiful tributes, and y'all know they are pitiful sometimes, to our amazing Black designers: Patrick Kelly, Willi Smith, Gordon Henderson, and the still standing Stephen Burrows. It will not be a salute to our mighty twentieth-century survivors: Tracy Reese, Byron Lars, Edward Wilkerson, and all the others still holding it down. This won't even be a nod to the new fashion kids on the Black block, even though I see you. Oh, I see you.

I am not going to praise how B-girls and round-the-way boys are the beginning and never-ending superheroes of fashion and youth style culture. I'm not even going to get down with the optimism energy and cool commerce the hip-hop generation brought to the entire fashion universe. How hip-hop style is something like a phenomenon, and how poor Black and Latino kids created a fashion revolution that rocked around the world. I'm not going to write about how door-knocker earrings knocked the cameo out the great American jewelry box. Or about how hip-hop style is like Michael Jackson, spanning generations because its innovation was fresh enough to outlive its originators. I won't tell the famous tale about how former hustlers made diamonds okay for day and denim fine for night, enough to make Jackie O clutch the pearls that everyone placed their this-is-high-American-style money on, and blew it because jeans and sneakers last longer and penetrate real people deeper than any pillbox hat and white gloves ever could.

Black style is not elitist, it's genius.

Shit, I'm not even going to talk about how only we organically and regularly weave fashion and style into our music, how Black people rap the best-dressed list, Jack. No, not even hip-hop is enough right now, and I believe hip-hop has the power to hurt and heal just about everything.

And, to take it all the way home, I'm not even going to tell a gritty and glamorous tale about growing up in Chocolate City: an odd-looking little light-bright Black girl with blond hair and green eyes, obsessed with paper dolls and fashion magazines. I'm not going to talk about the teenage girl who made clothes with her classmates and put on fashion shows for her friends; I'm not going to talk about how I had the most brilliant and marvelous auntie, who worked with legendary fashion photographers Richard Avedon and Hiro as the first Black stylist and then took me under her wing when I flew to New York to be with the fly girls and boys. How I went from theater to fashion, and launched magazines and a thousand stylish ships. How I grew to believe Black hair has power, genius, and magic in it, defying gravity and limitation. I mean, look at how marvelous it is: Black hair grows up and out. But there will be none of that now.

Sorry, kids, this ain't that kind of party—as a matter of fact, it ain't a party at all. This is a fight, a struggle of style to protect and secure our survival and legacy. Black style is *ours*. It belongs to *us*. We didn't throw it overboard with the diseases and the demons. We didn't get it kicked, choked, or raped out of us. It couldn't be burned up or shot up or locked up. You can't fuck it up.

Black style is indestructible, baby, and abuse and oppression only make it fresher.

Black style is our genius. We have finally made it to the generation that is baad and safe enough to holla and buck back if you try to take any more of our genius stuff. We are socially and intellectually armed and prepared to claim and defend our cultural and ancestral intangible jewels. We are the ones who recognize the high value of our style and beauty. We know our influence is beyond Black communities, that our style inspires and leads global conversations about image, power, and worth. We know how fierce we are and aren't afraid to let everyone know what we know.

We have crawled up a long and thorny runway to get here and have the scars to prove it and the stamina to get up and demand you understand: We do not require outside help to validate or promote the existence of Black cool, nor are we about to sit back and watch our cool be traded and consumed by those who have not worn the heavy cloak of the battered and beautiful Black burden. You can't try it on, or even pick it up. Our train of oppression is way too ornate and lengthy for you to bear. You need the height and majesty of generations of scattered collarbones to wear us. And besides, our history ain't for sale, either.

Fashion and style are a language and Black folk have a special patois that cannot be taught, borrowed, or bought. I know how style culture works: Ideas and images are out in the universe, transmitting through an illusive fashion frequency. There are those who can tune in and receive the precious privileged information. The messages are transmitted to the "style sensitives," also known as trendsetters, fashionistas, hipsters, and a slew of other names designed to separate the stylish from the sleepy. These messages are then communicated as unique hairstyles, beauty trends, and clever clothing creations and combinations. There are many insiders and innovators that can tap into what's next or what's hot. However, authentic Black style transmits on a funkier, flyer frequency that only Black folks can feel.

Black style and soul, it's not what you know or have. You can't prove it, you just feel it. I know it's frustrating, when your whole life you've been taught that information, intellect, and intelligence rule, right? Well, technically speaking,

Black style is a kind of intelligence. Having style, being cool, is something many Black folks have a high capacity for understanding, an ability to tap into a sophisticated frequency that registers not in the brain, but in the spirit.

Black style is not information or a combination of articles or labels—it is a feeling, like soul is a feeling.

Black cool is an intelligence of the soul.

Black American Style is a national treasure. It has delighted and dazzled the world's eyes, relieving the itch of the impending doom of the mainstream mundane. Black American Style is proof of human ingenuity, resilience, creativity and spirit.

From World War II zoot suits' causing riots to freedom hair's fighting the power during Civil Rights, Black style has told the honest story of our country's struggle and glory. It, like much of our music, has been celebrated and internationally imitated. The very idea that there are serious "Is There Black Style?" debates on college campuses, at design conferences, and in major mainstream media further tells the story.

What is it about Black style that makes other people want to own it, challenge it, and/or avoid it? It really must be something special, something of extreme value. Damn right it is. And the fact that only Black people really possess it, I think that really pisses off the privileged, all-power-to-the-information-and-access people. I'm talking about the ones who think they can buy or claim anything and if they cannot, they'll create words to justify taking more Black stuff, like "postracial" and "reverse racism."

True story: A top journalist for a top national newspaper suggested with the advent of Michelle Obama's wearing cardigans and designer clothes, that there is no distinct Black style and no need to distinguish it. Even some major Black media has drunk some of this wack Kool-Aid by placing non-Blacks in top fashion positions, deeming them qualified to define our style in our own house and represent Black style outside it. Questioning the existence of Black style and/or its relevance in some color-blind postracial-bullshit delusional debate should be considered culturally criminal or, better yet, irrelevant. I'd much rather ignore the ignorant shit, but, yet again, Black folks must always educate and illuminate before we eliminate and obliterate.

Just as brave Black people fought for the right to vote: *Black folks must fight to keep our cool.*

Some folks, white and Black, tried to have me wear that wack reverse-racism accessory when I challenged the notion that the one chair at the fashion front table labeled FASHION DIRECTOR reserved for Black women should be sat in by a Black woman. Race makes the most reasonable arguments complicated. If I were saying a straight woman shouldn't represent the image of gay men, I wouldn't be called a reverse anything. It's a clear position. Yet because this was an injustice of image representation because of race, it was offensive.

I am not responsible for "others'" ignorance or denial about race or white privilege. I no longer carry the burden of navigating other people's feelings. I will not be quiet for any one else's comfort. That's it. No more explanation and no negotiation, and yes, I am ready to fight. Black style, our cool, is precious, worthy of protecting, defending, and being accountable to. Enough taking and enough giving away.

The worst part about defending the right for a Black woman to lead the style of a magazine for Black women was the fact that I was in a position of defense in the first place. Who gives away their legacy and calls it equal opportunity? What group of people would even entertain relinquishing their cool in some misguided molested attempt at cultural progress and integration? The image industry is not equal or integrated, not even close, and it's disrespectful to Black history, struggle, and dignity to pretend it is. Who else in our culture negotiates their image, cuts deals with their history?

Are the few Black folks in the big houses of style so desperate for acceptance or disappearance that they are unwilling or afraid to declare, "The negotiation with Black cool and mainstream media are a fucking ripoff"? Who else compromises with their presence? Let's take a look at what these deals tend to look like: Society agrees Paris Hilton coined the term "That's hot" and Bo Derek made cornrows hot; Black-cool culture gets what in return? Here's another negotiation: If there can be just one Black model at a time walking among the legions of white models on the runway, we promise not to cause a scene because using one fucking Black model equals diversity in a privileged crazy-ass white world? So who's crazy? The ones who think they are diversity practitioners or those who accept it as true diversity? The answer is both.

It's time to move from fighting the power to fighting for the power.

This is a subtle yet substantial twist in the struggle for total equality and justice. The time has come when we cease being satisfied with Black presence being sprinkled about (Diddy, I see you). I'm not saying it's not a beautiful thing that some Black folks of style have made it into the room; some of us even make the room (I see you, Michelle Obama). Yet even when a Black president and an exquisite Black First Lady have power and presence, there is not one major publication or television show dedicated to Black fashion and style. Nor do mainstream style outlets employ enough Blacks or consistently use Black images.

I know for white folks it's tricky—one Black face can upset the delicate balance. It can distract from the intended fantasy of purity and perfection. Blackness interjects an entirely different fantasy; one Black face among twenty others can shift pristine to passionate with no effort. Blackness disrupts and distracts. Look at how Black exaggerated exoticism has been sold and re-sold for centuries, and how society has been complicit with impressive discipline in the absence of explicitly Black cool from all things publicly glamorous. And, of course, there is the wildly successful image campaign promoting Black sexual deviance and societal and cultural inferiority, creating the popular notion that Black chicks are not only not chic, but pitiful and dirty. Who wants a broke-down welfare queen or an ill-proportioned video ho on their glossy pages or immaculate runways?

It's not all white folks' fault. Yes, they create, promote, and, most sadly, believe many of the narrow images projected are the Black norm, but what about Black folks? What have Black folks done to counterbalance the dangerous, stifling, and false images? What images have Black people added to the twisted fantasy and disappearance of Black beauty? What happened in the last decade that many Blacks who create or consume style have become so passive or destructive? How will anyone learn or remember the genius of Black cool if Black folks themselves don't relentlessly interject interesting, innovative, incredible images into the collective cultural imagination?

Black people cannot continue to make themselves so easy to ignore, and they must keep what they have buoyant and relevant. What that means is: Black folks must keep the pressure on mainstream fashion media to include Black style and not just use it when it suits the season. And for the Black media that are still alive, we must keep the pressure on them to be excellent and stop giving away what little cultural cachet we have. Black folks have to stop being afraid to be real Black. Time to stop simmering down the heat of Black cool in order to make white folks comfortable. Rather, Black folks need to keep the temperature up so everyone can get accustomed to the heat. Black image-makers have to remember it is the heat in Black cool that's hot and heals.

We cannot forget the fearlessness of the Black style icons and everyday fly folk who risked acceptance and employment to proudly present their clothes, their face, or their hair in styles that countered the imbalance of the mainstream. Black style tells the truth about the Black imagination. It's walking proof of the genius. The exposure of the power, depth, and beauty of the Black imagination can be dangerous in a time when acceptance in the eyes of the big beholder seems so sweet. The tragic truth is that Black acceptance in a protected white existence is temporal and easily disposable, so when Black folks are invited to the party, they might as well bring the noise.

Here is the best news: No matter what anyone does or doesn't do, Black cool never dies, because it was never born. It is a gift given before time to a people who would know exactly how to play with it. God gave cool to the people from the hot continent. Neither greedy men nor hungry women can ever own it or destroy it. This is how it works: Humankind must be responsible for divine gifts. It's how we stay involved in creation. We have seen the mayhem that can occur when Black folks allow the cultural and intellectual siphoning and theft of our imagination. To witness, as I have, a high-end fashion show inspired entirely by hip-hop, down to the dookie chains and door knockers, without one Black or Latino model on the catwalk is a crime against culture.

Let Black style be the phenomenal cultural jewel it is, set respectfully and unmolested in the great crown of global style. Society and especially Black folks must see Black style as the Holy Grail it is, worthy of valiant defense throughout all ages. Black style is magic, a mystical energy that emanated out of ancient Africa and waited for an eternity for a people worthy of embodying it. The people came. From Nefertari to Nina Simone to Naomi Campbell to Nicki Minaj, they came to bear witness to the power of the gift. Black style is our spiritual birthright, not to be borrowed or bargained against, ever.

Forgive me y'all for the strong words, but when Black style is threatened, forgotten, or questioned, I lose my cool.

FOREVER
bell
hooks

In a basket in my tiny New York flat in the West Village I have a picture of the young Miles Davis cut from a newspaper with a caption that reads: "Cool is forever." I was obsessed with the idea of "cool" in my girlhood, an idea that came into my life from grown Black men who listened to jazz, dressed sharp, and called me "doll" with know-it-all intimacy.

When I left small-town rural America headed for California, I was on my way to the Bay Area, seeking an education for sure but also looking for the world of cool I had read about in the words of the Beat poets. Sitting on the floor of City Lights bookstore, listening to Yevtushenko read to a packed audience, among a silence so intense that it was as though we had all come together in a moment of prayer, I remember thinking, *This is it—the place of cool.*

Again and again I found that cool in small clubs, listening to Cecil Taylor or Ornette Coleman, listening to all the hip, culturally aware men talk about hearing Coltrane live at the Blue Note. When I did the cooking for a local jazz club I had an all-night firsthand look at cool and it was soon clear to me that the males, no matter their color, saw the world of cool as masculine. In the world of cool, females were mere backup singers.

The sexual revolution and women's liberation changed all that. And I was right there on the spot, eager to take my place among the cool. As all the revolutions happened women began to move from behind the scenes in the world of music and showed that talent, genius, was not gendered. Whether I was listening to early Laura Nyro (with Patti LaBelle singing in the background) or seeing Alice Coltrane jam in a local park, it was for me a moment of arrival; women were there in the art scene, there in the poetry and music worlds, forging their own place of cool.

All through the years from my twenties into the forties, I was confident that I possessed the cool that is forever. But as my hair began to gray and my bones grew weary and still, as I entered the midlife world of successful fifty-year-old folk all settled and comfortable, I began to doubt.

Soon I will be sixty and I have to work harder to imagine there is a place for me in the continuing world of cool. Aging men coming from the world of the streets, the world of subcultures, and all manner of art making always seem to find recognition that they are still cool. They can don the clothes of a youthful male generation as sign and symbol that they are still hip, still hanging out in the magical world of cool. The last time I went to a Meshell Ndegeocello concert in a Brooklyn warehouse they were all there, these older men, rapping to girls young enough to be their grandchildren. When I walked the space it was clear that there were not many women over fifty in the crowd. And truth be told, I am often alone among women my age in my continued obsession with being cool.

In 2011, I made the decision to leave New York, to sell the 340-square-feet studio in the West Village. Making home-place in a small town in Kentucky, I began to fret about the possibility of losing all claims to cool. And then the insight that cool is forever pushed its way to the fore and I planted trees on a devastated Kentucky hill and talked to the native ancestors who clearly understood the word of style and cool, and don't I have the artifacts handed down to show the essential coolness of their world? And did I not sit at the feet of the aging poet Gwendolyn Brooks and hear her recite her "We Real Cool" poem with as much vigor and passion as when I first heard her when she was younger and I was just stepping out of girlhood and claiming my grown-up-woman self? The phrase "we real cool" became the title of the book I wrote on masculinity, and led to the following meditation:

Once upon a time Black male "cool" was defined by the ways in which Black men confronted the hardships of life without allowing their spirits to be ravaged. They took the pain of it and used it alchemically to turn the pain into gold. That burning process required high heat. Black male cool was defined by the ability to withstand the heat and remain centered. It was defined by Black male willingness to confront reality, to face the truth, and bear it not by adopting a false pose of cool while feeding on fantasy; not by Black male denial, but by individual Black males daring to self-define rather than be defined by others.

Using their imaginations to transcend all the forms of oppression that would keep them from celebrating life, individual Black males created a context where they can be self-defining and transform a world beyond themselves. Critic Stanley Crouch attests to this power in *The All-American Skin Game, or, the Decoy of Race* when he talks about Louis Armstrong:

> *Lifting his trumpet to a scarred embouchure, he rose from the gumbo pot of the Western Hemisphere like a brown Poseidon of melody. Armstrong was then calling up the heroic, Afro-American lyricism of hope swelling out beyond deep recognition of tragedy, and was also enriching our ambivalent sense of adult romance through the beat of the matchless dance in which all of the complexities of courtship and romantic failure seem to have located themselves in the Argentinian steps of endless ballroom couples so expressive of passion nuance they seem forever mythic. The transcending power of such combinations is symbolic of the affirmative, miscegenated heat necessary to melt down the iron suits of history.*

If every young Black male in America simply studied the history, the life, and work of Black musicians, they would have the blueprints for healing and survival. They would see clearly the roads they can take that will lead to a life of suffering and pain and the roads they can take that will lead to paradise, to healing, to a life lived in community.

In the opening statement of his autobiography, *Blues All Around Me*, B.B. King declares: "When it comes to my own life, others may know the cold facts better than me . . . Truth is, cold facts don't tell the whole story . . . I'm not writing a cold-blooded history. I'm writing a memory of my heart. That's the truth I'm after—following my feelings no matter where they lead. I want to try to understand myself, hoping that you . . . will understand me as well."

Sharing what the blues meant to him as a boy, King states, "Blues meant hope, excitement, pure emotion. Blues were about feelings." Just as today's gangsta rap invites Black males to adopt a cool pose, to front and fake it, to mask true feelings, the blues was an invitation to Black men to be vulnerable, to express true feelings, to break open their hearts and expose them. Black males have helped create the blues, more than any other music, as a music of resistance to the patriarchal notion that a real man should never express genuine feelings. Emotional awareness of real-life pain in Black men's lives was and is the heart and soul of the blues. When the guitar player sings, "I found a leak in my building, and my soul has got to move. I say my soul has got to move," he is singing about the pain of betrayal, about the soul's need not to be abandoned, but to find shelter in a secure emotional place.

It is no accident that one of the moments of heartbreak in the career of B. B. King happened at a sixties concert where he confronted a world that was turning away from the blues.

A new generation of Black folks wanted to dance and swing, to party and do their thing—a generation that did not want to deal with the pain of the past or of the present. King remembers:

> *The sixties were filled with beautiful soul because Black people were more vocal about the respect we wanted and the good feeling we had about ourselves. The politics seeped into the music, and the politics were about life-affirming change.*

Had these politics been truly liberating they would have embraced the blues as a powerful legacy of Black male redemption. Instead, King recalls:

> *We want to get ahead. But in pushing ahead, sometimes we resent the old forms of music. They represent a time we'd rather forget, a period of history where we suffered shame and humiliation. Makes no difference that the blues is an expression of anger against shame or humiliation. In the minds of many young Blacks the blues stood for a time and place they'd outgrown.*

This contempt for powerful legacies of Black male identity in resistance set the stage for the hip-hop generation's disdain for the emotional complexity of Black male experience.

No wonder, then, that most hip-hop culture offers Black males very little "real" spiritual nourishment. Sure, it may teach them to play the dominator game, and sure, they may play all the way to wealth. But it does not teach them how to move beyond gaming to find the place of soulfulness, of being, of a cool that is about being well in your soul, being real.

Speaking of keeping it real, Todd Boyd writes in *The New H.N.I.C.*:

> *The Death of Civil Rights and the Reign of Hip Hop,* *"Hip hop is concerned on the other hand with being 'real,' honoring the truth of one's own convictions, while refusing to bend over to accommodate the dictates of the masses. Unlike the previous generation of people who often compromised or made do, in search of something bigger, hip-hop sees compromise as false, fake, and bogus."*

This idea of being "real" sounds more like a warmed-over version of white patriarchal masculinity's notion that a "real man" proves his manhood by remaining rigidly attached to his position, refusing to change. It reveals the emotional immaturity that underlies much hip-hop sentiment. Ironically, Boyd mocks the mature struggles for social justice, like civil rights, that made it possible for the hip-hop generation to bop their way forward without suffering significant racist assault and repression; he states unself-consciously, "In the same way that civil rights spoke to the conditions back in the day, hip hop artists now speak to a populace often disillusioned by those considered overtly political in a traditional sense." Much hip-hop culture is mainstream because it is just a Black minstrel show—an imitation of dominator desire, not a rearticulation, not a radical alternative. It is not surprising, then, that patriarchal hip-hop culture has done little to save the lives of Black males and done more to teach them that the vision of "we real cool" includes the assumption that "we die soon"—an observation Gwendolyn Brooks made in her poem "We Real Cool." Brooks saw the need to critique this vision of cool that was connected to self-destruction decades ago.

Boyd's definition of cool links it to the state of being lifeless, to necrophilia: "Cool is about a detached, removed, nonchalant sense of being. An aloofness that suggests one is above it all. Pride, an arrogance even, that is at once laid back, unconcerned, perceived to be highly sexual and potentially violent." This definition of Black male cool rearticulates the way unenlightened white male hipsters read Black masculinity. It is a stereotyped notion of cool that denies the history of the "real cool," which was not about disassociation, hardheartedness, and violence, but rather about being intensely connected, aware, and able to judge the right action to take in a given circumstance. Boyd's commonplace version of Black male cool defines it in terms that mirror the traits of sociopaths and psychopaths; it's all about disassociation. As such it is a vision of Black masculinity that merely reinforces the status quo and offers no possibilities of redemptive change or healing. It is the ultimate drug that keeps Black men addicted to the status quo and in their place.

Though Boyd, and many of his cronies, like to think that calling themselves "niggas" and basking in the glory of gangsta culture, glamorizing addiction to drugs, pussy, and material things, is liberation, they personify the spiritual zombiehood of today's "cool" Black male. They have been bought with a price; they are not their own. And the sad fact is that they do not even know they are faking and fronting while mouthing off about keeping it real; they bring new meaning to the word *denial*. In actuality the culture they promote is all about playing dead and loving it, or being dead and leaving behind a legacy of death.

Even though popular culture has made the Black male body and presence stand for the apex of "cool," it is a death-dealing coolness, not one that is life enhancing, for Black males or the folks they associate with. Young males embrace a notion of cool that is about getting pussy and getting ready to kill (or at least making somebody think they can kill), because as an identity this one is easier to come by than the quest to know the self and to create a life of meaning. Right now in our nation not enough adult Black males chart the path to healthy self-esteem for younger Black males. That path requires self-acceptance, assuming accountability, letting go of the politics of blame, telling the truth, and being positive.

In the wake of the militant sixties, the patriarchal Black Power movement ushered in a politics of cool that was all about dominator culture, asserting power in the very ways righteous Black men had criticized from the moment they touched earth in the so-called new world. This notion of cool was all about exploitation, the con, the hustle, getting over, getting by. Even though it dumped on the white man, it was all about being the white man, with all the perks and goodies that come with patriarchal dominator power. Not surprisingly, then, these Black males had no respect for a notion of cool that was predicated upon their ability to use their prophetic imaginations to transcend the politics of domination and create beloved community. Patriarchal notions of cool have diminished the spirit of Black male creativity; they have contained and in many cases crushed Black male imagination.

Real cool, the cool that is forever, stirs the imagination.

HUNGER
VERONICA
CHAMBERS

Appetite, like so many elements of Black cool, is a double-edged sword. Our appetite for the new, delicious, and fresh can bring us great joy: physical, emotional, mental. There are few culinary terms more elegant than "soul food." Google the terms "soul food" and "yoga," or "soul food" and "spirituality," and the four million–plus results for each search are a powerful reminder that when people—Black, white, and everything in between—think of the term "soul food," they are looking for much more than the hours and directions to Sylvia's Sunday gospel brunch in Harlem.

And yet as a people, our relationship to appetite, our gut desire to be fed something good, runs the gamut from joyful to painful, unheralded, and complicated. Zora Neale Hurston once wrote, "I been in sorrow's kitchen and licked out all the pots. Then I have stood on the peaky mountain wrapped in rainbows, with a harp and a sword in my hands." I think it's telling how often only the first part of that quote is repeated, as if sorrow were the only kitchen that existed—then and now, for us as a people.

I've been thinking a lot about food in part because of the unbridled success of Marcus Samuelsson's restaurant, the Red Rooster. Marcus has been a friend for a long time—and it's with him that I've had some of my most interesting "food conversations"—a term that Marcus uses a lot that references not only the meal, but the cook, the diner, and the setting.

My earliest intellectual knowledge that those four elements could come together in a powerful way was in college, when I read hungrily, greedily, super-size-my-portion-style, about the Harlem Renaissance. I was smitten at once with the story of A'Lelia Bundles, daughter of Madam C. J. Walker. If Madam C. J. Walker was the first American woman to become a self-made millionaire, then A'Lelia Bundles was the first Black socialite (and I mean that in the best sense of the word—encompassing both the gift of being social and the gift of being light in spirit). Langston Hughes called Bundles the "joy goddess" of Harlem; her home on 136th Street was the site of many a legendary meal.

Bundles had a voracious appetite not only for the gatherings that can surround great food, but for the very Harlem Renaissance-era hunger for all that was *new*. One might even argue that she orchestrated the first culinary mash-up when she invited her white guests to dine on chitlins and bathtub gin in the kitchen while her Black guests feasted on caviar and champagne in the formal dining room.

Another tale about the joy goddess was that one night, the crowds outside her townhouse were so thick that the prince of Sweden couldn't make his way through. There was no red carpet or velvet rope chez Bundles; the gracious hostess simply sent down her regards to visiting royalty, along with a bottle of champagne. CP time would not do if you wanted to be part of the food conversations at Mademoiselle Bundles' swanky salons. As Langston Hughes wrote in his autobiography, "Unless you were early, there was no possible way of getting in . . . Her parties were as crowded as the New York subway at rush hour."

As a college student stuck in the Berkshire woods, longing for community and food conversation, I noted that many believed that the Harlem Renaissance's official launch could be dated to a dinner: March 21, 1924, at a civic club affair for Charles Johnson's magazine *Opportunity*. Although I never learned what the attendees were served, I do know that the meal featured "white critics whom 'everybody' knew and Negro writers whom 'nobody' knew meeting on common ground." Among the nobodies were all the somebodies I had studied and admired: Countee Cullen and Langston Hughes, Jessie Fauset and Alain Locke, who formally presented his take on "the New Negro."

There were more books to be written and more chances to break bread. On May 1, 1925, the Opportunity Awards dinner was held at the Fifth Avenue Restaurant, on the corner of Twenty-fourth Street. Attendees included Paul Robeson, Arthur Schomburg, Fannie Hurst, and many others. Just a few

weeks after the dinner, where Langston Hughes presented se-
lections from *The Weary Blues*—soul food on the menu, if not
literally, then spiritually—Hughes received his first contract
for a book of poetry, from Knopf.

I threw my first dinner parties—with no sense of scope or
the limitations of budget—inspired by those mythic Opportunity dinners. I boldly invited friends I loved and strangers
I admired over to eat at my house, hungry for the kind of inspiring interactions that I had read about. Sue Mengers, the
first female superagent in Hollywood, threw legendary dinner parties. She once said, "On a scale of 1 to 10, I'd say that
entertaining has contributed 5 to my success. It is harder for
someone to screw you if they've had dinner at your house."
This, I learned, is not true. But I have spent days and nights
and mornings making food for the most amazing people, and
the resulting conversations have fed my confidence, my curi-
osity, my work, and my worldview in innumerable ways.

This will make me sound old, older even than I am, but
I think it's bad form, the amount of recent college grads who
think that they are cultivating me as a mentor by pinging
me endlessly on every social-media platform imaginable.
I still believe a lunch, a dinner, even a quick conversation
over a cup of Starbucks tea, will make more of an impact
on me than the most artfully worded email. Maya Angelou
once said that "when people show you who they are, believe
them—the first time." I guess the problem for me is that it's

hard for me to really gauge who people *are* online, while food, even when we don't prepare the meal, allows us to show a little of ourselves.

I believe in the power of travel to elevate and expand, but food offers a great deal of opportunity to journey, too. In 1992, when John Singleton asked me to come to L.A. to work on a book about the making of his sophomore film, *Poetic Justice*, I ended up moving into a short-term residency in Koreatown (loooong story.) About a month after I moved in, the L.A. riots happened and I sat in my apartment for days, afraid and under siege, with no one but a bunch of Korean businessmen raiding the same vending machines for sustenance. I didn't leave Koreatown, but instead made a deeper effort to really get to know the community. I visited a Korean restaurant, had the seafood *pa jun*, and fell into a kind of love that led, in twists and turns, to my having a cadre of Korean friends, reading Korean short stories, even traveling to Seoul. My own sense of what was cool, my Bundles-like appetite for what was new, was like so many Black women's before me: birthed during a moment of struggle, but nurtured in the light.

Another interesting thing about appetite is that it is tied so deeply to possibility: It is hard to hunger for something you've never had, be it a trip abroad, something as indescribable as unconditional love, or an exquisite seven-course meal. When I first met Marcus, he was still at Aquavit and he either had just become or was about to become the youngest chef to receive three Michelin stars. I'd written my first book, *Mama's Girl*, and was going through my own hoops as youngest and first this or that. Marcus invited me to come to the restaurant with a friend for a seven-course tasting dinner, paired with wine.

For me it was a night of many firsts—my first seven-course meal, my first meal paired with wine, my first pickled herring, my first foie gras, my first sashimi, my first barolo, my first riesling, and on and on. I was never the same, and not just because I then became the (ever so slightly high maintenance) Black girl who asked prospective dates to meet me at the bar at Aquavit for black Angus sliders and a glass of spirits infused with mango, chili, and lime—more because I understood why fine dining was worth the hefty price tag: A tasting dinner is an invitation to experience the imagination of a great chef, to literally taste the world in a different way.

I resolved to have a tasting dinner—all five or six or seven luxurious courses—once a year, at the very minimum. I've been fortunate enough to have tasting dinners all over the world, from Australia to South Africa. And just as I know that I owe it to Marcus for giving me that critical exposure, I also know that somewhere A'Lelia Bundles was toasting me with a glass of heaven's best champagne.

We should support our Black chefs like we support our Black movies, flood their reservation lines the way we line Tyler Perry's pockets every time he says, "Madea," go and visit the culinary temples of great chefs like Leah Chase, G. Garvin, Govind Armstrong, and, of course, Marcus's Red Rooster and his downtown outpost, August. But the moral of the story can't be that we should all be so lucky as to have an exquisite meal at a wonderful restaurant cooked by a great Black chef.

There's a next chapter in our dining that is just as important as the great galas of the Harlem menus, that is just as vital as our beloved traditions of kitchen-table wisdom and diverse dinners where debate is as much a part of the meal as anything being served on a dish. The very term "soul food" was meant to describe food that nourished us—and we know well that too many of our people, too many of our young people, are not eating foods that nourish their body or their intellect or their soul. I hesitate to take to the pulpit, because it's a journey of mindfulness that I am on, too, but I think it's worthwhile to share the journey even before you get to your destination.

Our appetite—our hunger, both literal and metaphorical—can also hold us back. We've got to start eating more whole foods and less junk foods. We need more farmers' markets in our neighborhoods, and we need to believe that a drive to get delectable ingredients is as worthy as a drive to the mall. We've got to demand more of what we put into our bodies and ask ourselves, *Is this a dish that will feel as good as it tastes?* And as we embark on this process of reinventing soul food for the twenty-first century, we've got to take someone along with us. Each one, teach one: a sister, a cousin, a niece, a nephew, or a friend.

I recently took a sista friend I adore with me to Rancho La Puerta, a spa in Mexico, that is one of my very favorite happy places. Everything there is grown within just a few short miles, and the chefs cook with very little saturated fat and a whole lot of love. On the second evening of our stay, my friend and I signed up for the silent dinner and sat underneath a trellis of hot-pink plumeria, eating a meal of salad greens garnished with edible blossoms, puréed gazpacho topped with diced yellow tomatoes, perfectly seared salmon and grilled vegetables, and, for dessert, a platter of berries that shone like jewels. We spent the entire dinner in silence, and I hoped that my friend could somehow intuit all that I couldn't say: *You are big and beautiful, but you are not big and healthy. Be good to yourself, because you're the only you I've got. Let's take on the health issues you've been facing, no shame or blame, one dish at a time. You rock those designer handbags, but food that sustains you is a worthier luxury.*

These days, I throw far fewer dinner parties than I used to (although I will say that our Juneteenth party was slamming—freedom tastes *good*). More often than not, I cook for an audience of two: my daughter and my husband. August Wilson used to wash his hands, like Pontius Pilate, before writing. I wash my hands before cooking and let the moments of warm water and lathering soap become a sort of meditation: *Help me, Lord, not to oversalt this frittata, because you know my hand has a tendency to be heavy. Please let this be the day when my daughter asks for four servings of broccoli, like that day that was so unreal that I think I must have dreamt it. Let this meal be a way for me to show, not tell, my love. Let these pots and all they are capable of conjuring sustain my little family the way my grandmother's rice and beans sustained me—through sickness and in health, for better and for worse and hopefully mostly for better, forever and forever. Amen.*

ECCENTRICITY

MARGO JEFFERSON

I.

First of all, I intend to say *Negro* rather than *Black*. *Negro* is eccentric now. Removed from the orbit of high-end racial brand names like *Black* or *African American*, always popping up in pointed or playful ways to inflect, add the overtone or undertone, the historical aside to our discourse.

Every few decades our names shift. But *Black* and *African American* aim at a stability that serves social and political ends. *Negro* reflects all the instabilities, all the circumstances, imposed on us. And by us.

Long before the *nigger/nigga* usage debate, *Negro* was doing multiple duties in terms of meaning and implication. It could be august and mighty, as when A. Philip Randolph said, "Negro Principles Are Not For Sale"; rueful but affectionate, as when one exclaims, "My Negroes!" upon encountering some name, hairdo, or action that runs the gamut from ingenious to entertaining to embarrassing; chivalric, as when we sing the Negro national anthem or speak of Negro life and history.

II.

Eccentricity the word and eccentricity the concept have long been linked to our history as a people. European astronomers first used the term to describe a planetary orbit that didn't have the earth precisely at its center. That was in the sixteenth century, just as European rulers were busy claiming and naming off-center orbits in the Caribbean and the Americas.

Now consider the word *kink*, which will eventually become a synonym for *eccentricity*. (Actually, let's say "synonymical partner," in the spirit of Black verbal eccentricity, which revels in grandeur.) The word *kink*, meaning "twist in a rope," appeared in English in the 1670s, thanks to the Dutch, who were also busy claiming their own off-center orbits in North America. The age of reason saw its meaning expand to include odd and unusual behavior, odd and unusual individuals, mental twists and twisted outcomes. In 1852 Harriet Beecher Stowe (from whom our destiny as a people cannot be sundered) put it in *Uncle Tom's Cabin*. A slave mother whose son has just been bought by a slave trader pleads with the trader:

"'Buy me too, Mas'r, for de dear Lord's sake!—buy me,—I shall die if you don't!'

"'You'll die if I do, that's the kink of it,' said Haley—'no!' And he turned on his heel."

That's the kink of it, all right—the twist, the flaw, the killer irony, and the lethal fault line of Negro life in the United States. How was it that almost exactly one hundred years later, *kink* had become a belittling word for the twists, knots, and naps in our hair—a potent physical sign, to white Americans, of our degraded eccentricity?

III.

Zora Neale Hurston's now celebrated 1934 essay, "Characteristics of Negro Expression," was, in fact, about characteristics of Negro eccentricity. Orbits of behavior, action, reaction that did not have bourgeois Anglo-Saxon culture at their center. Speech, movement, music, sculpture, interior design, everyday ways of being.

An important legacy of that essay is this: We must constantly, continually reassess the forms Negro eccentricity takes. Plenty of these forms are sanctioned now, thanks to generations of artists and scholars who were resourceful and committed enough to know how easily eccentricity can be seen as ignorance and vulgarity—a cause of acute social embarrassment. And, like any form developing in the moment, working at the ground level of culture, it experiments wantonly and makes what each of us considers big mistakes. (Young Negro men in pants hanging significantly below their butts? Big mistake.)

I used to declare absurd those long, curved acrylic nails in loud colors and designs favored by young Negro women, especially when the women were doing things like bagging groceries and hitting cash registers all day. I still don't like most of them. But they're no more absurd than talons or decorated shields. Aggressively functional, visually commanding. As Hurston wrote of the "glut" of decoration she saw in the homes of "the average Negro": "Grotesque? Yes. But it indicated a desire for beauty . . . The feeling back of such an act is that there can never be enough beauty, let alone too much." Beauty. Snap. Killer pizzazz. The look that will turn heads and make jaws drop in the supermarket, in the subway car, or on the street—there can never be enough of that. "What are you going to wear?" I once asked a friend. "I'm going to be overdressed, as usual," she answered serenely. And there we have our Eccentric Principles of Negro Dress. We favor the sublimely, absurdly, breathtakingly overdressed.

And we have left our mark on fashion history. Some of my favorite examples from decades past: white vinyl gladiator sandals (worn by young women); spandex shorts in electric yellow, red, blue, or white, with matching tank tops and stocking caps knotted at the nape of the neck (worn by young gay men with perfect bodies); Little Bo Peep knit caps with a ruffle framing the face (worn for a season in Chicago by adult, apparently hetero men of all shapes and sizes. An error, I think. But a bold error: Black manhood courting— flaunting—the girlishness of the British nursery rhyme).

IV.

We are all proud of our people's contribution to the English language, their centuries of vernacular resourcefulness. How we creatively disrupt and rework grammar, syntax, and diction, devise new words and revise old ones. I'm especially fond of how we join formality with dissonance. The formality comes from the words chosen, the dissonance from how they are combined and what they describe. A few celebrity examples:

Larry Holmes, on the fact that he did time in prison: "I had the misfortune to fight a man who expired later on."

Don King, referring to one or another triumph: "I feel gratification beyond description or depiction."

Gilbert Arenas, on his decision to bring several of his guns into the Wizards' locker room: "I wasn't using longevity thinking."

I often enjoy the way we add *s*'s to proper nouns, as in "I love that little Robert Downey Juniors," which manages to suggest the scattered actions of his drug-addled years, along with his uncanny ability to slip in and out of accents and personae.

And—standard, even banal, as it can be—our adding -*ass* to nouns and adjectives always works in the hands of a talented speaker or writer. Who could better Bassey Ikpi's tweet description of the dapper and self-satisfied Usher as "meerkat-ass-looking"?

Likewise, our way of adding syllables to words where none have gone before. The purpose? To suggest other words and ideas, to fatten up the sound pleasurably. When *voluptuous* becomes *volumptuous*, intimations of *plump, voluminous, sumptuous,* and even *heffalumptuous* (a shout-out here to A. A. Milne) are at play.

We like to chop syllables off words, too, but the effect is elliptical rather than curt. *Zo* and *Gyptian* sound faintly extraterrestrial. *Trife* (from *trifling*) and *bable* (from *probablement*) are enigmatic rather than explicit. Eccentricity is a mode of protective coloration. A declaration of cultural independence.

When in the Course of human events, it becomes necessary for one people to dissolve the cultural standards which have injuriously connected them with another and to assume among the powers of the earth, the separate and equal station to which the Laws of Cultural History entitle them, then they must hold these truths to be self-evident: that all peoples are endowed with certain unalienable rights and among these are innovation, improvisation, and variation.

V.

Surely this must be what drives Negro nomenclature, the drive behind our insatiable need to invent new names for ourselves, names that address and fracture, incorporate history and myth and the fetishes of media and consumer culture.

I offer here some recent successes. And I put them in capital letters to give them the majesty, the opulence, the *volumptuousness* their creators desired.

CLASSICAL ALLUSIONS:

ETHELLO FERGUSON

CYMONISSE AND CIEMONE

TREMARIUS CAMPBELL

POP-CULTURE HEROES:
D'ALCAPONE ALPACCINO MORRIS
SALMINEO WEBSTER

As a friend who observed a little girl at the Estée Lauder counter of Saks exuberantly crying, "That's my name, that's my name!" while pointing to one Clinique product after another said, "Once you're five-fifths of a woman, you can do anything you want with nomenclature."

SOUL
HANK
WILLIS
THOMAS

What is soul? I don't know! Soul is a ham hock in your corn flakes. What is soul? I don't know! Soul is ashy ankles and rusty kneecaps! What is soul? I don't know! Soul is the ring around your bathtub!

> *What is soul? Soul is you, baby. Soul is you!*

—Funkadelic

The generation before me was defined by soul. Soul was a virtue born out of the spirituality of gospel, the pain of blues, and the progressive pride of being the standard-bearers of civil rights. They were stylish like Shaft, but noble like Martin. They sang on Sunday mornings, after "sangin'" on Saturday nights. They pressed their thrift store suits with so much starch that the bare-threaded knees were as stiff as if they'd just bought them new at Brooks Brothers. Almost everyone was poor, so there wasn't any shame in it.

Not my generation. We were defined by "cool," an emotionally detached word that provokes a cold response to the world with a narrowly focused ambition for its ice, its bling, and its things. We heard stories of our parents and grandparents fighting for the right to be fully recognized Americans. We saw some folks from the neighborhood come up—way up. They became ballers, rappers, hustlers, actors—even a few doctors and lawyers. On TV we saw it happening right before our eyes: the Jeffersons, the Cosbys, Jesse Jackson running for president, and Michael Jackson, Michael Jordan, Magic Johnson, and Whitney Houston dominating the airwaves.

But the majority of us saw the dreams, passions, and hopes of our parents dashed by the regression of a Black community linked to the welfare system, project housing, rising unemployment, deteriorating education, addiction, and an increase in Black men in the penal system. *Good Times* and *What's Happening!!* were funny in the 1970s, but by the eighties they were in reruns and the joke seemed to be on us.

Something broke in the community spirit of my generation. "Easy credit rip-offs" and "scratchin' and survivin'"[1] didn't add up to "good times" anymore, so we rejected soul and turned back to cool. But not that Miles Davis, John Coltrane kind of cool. That was too old school. We became fully legitimate Americans—capitalists—more concerned with getting that money and "My Adidas" than being "Kind of Blue" and singing "We Shall Overcome." Nobody was makin' it talking about "we"—it was all about "me." Civil rights slogans like "I am a man" were adapted for the hip-hop audience to say, "I am *the* man." Our community focus shifted inward—everyone was out for self. We were primed, and corporate America was prepared for our long-awaited integration into mainstream American commerce.

In 1981, I got my first pair of Nike shoes. It was around this same time I learned that I was "Black." At the time, I saw no connection between the two. I was only five years old, and statistically more likely to be dead or in jail by twenty-one than to be in college. But I didn't know anything about that; I just knew that I liked the color blue. So when my mom got me blue canvas shoes with blue suede patches at the toe and heel and white leather Swooshes on both sides, I just stared at them in amazement. Something about them was special.

One night, as we rode on a graffiti-covered New York City subway train, I asked my mother, "What does the word on the back mean? Nike?" She didn't know. I asked, "What does the white design on the sides of the shoes mean?" She didn't know the answer to that, either.[2]

Though I asked a lot of questions in those days, I never asked my mother what being "Black" meant, even though I was becoming more aware daily that I was branded with that label, too. In retrospect, I doubt she could have explained that, either. At that age, I didn't yet see the connection between getting my first label and discovering my racial label. I was unaware of advertising, semiotics, peer pressure, *cool*, or even racism. Now I marvel at the depth of the significance of my childhood fascination with a simple visual symbol, so cool that it motivated a generation to be its flag bearers.

There's no way to prove it, but I would argue that almost every urban American child from the 1980s remembers the first time he or she heard of Michael Jordan or his shoes. I will never forget when I first saw them: Nike's Air Jordans. It was 1985, and my mother and I were at a Foot Locker in a New Jersey mall. All I can remember thinking was, *Wha... ?! How could they make such a shoe?* They were high-top sneakers with a drawing of a winged basketball on the back and Nike Swooshes on each side. As if the style were not cool enough, the store display rocked my nine-year-old world with a giant poster of a Black man wearing the red shoes, frozen in midair! With echoes of Michael Jackson's moonwalk in my mind, I marveled, *They can make you fly!* Just like that, I'd been indoctrinated into the cult of cool.

Each year, when the new model of Air Jordans was introduced, every Black kid I knew, rich or poor, was trying to get those "sneaks." A crisp, clean pair of brand-spanking-new Air Jordan sneakers was a supreme status symbol for anyone who wanted to be cool and "down with the streets." One kid could be heard saying to another, "Yo! Did you see the new Jordans? Them joints is fly, yo!" A typical response would be "Yeah, man, I got them on layaway" or "They're fresh, but I still like last year's better!" The latter was code for "my mom can't afford them."

The average outsider looking around the projects or a dilapidated inner-city neighborhood might not even have imagined that teenagers were wearing shoes that cost nearly the equivalent of an entire month's rent. The visitor might have wondered, *Why not trade the shoes in and move to a better neighborhood?* But that would have defeated the purpose of buying the shoes. The point was to be in the *concrete jungle* and dress like a million bucks. That defiance was the essence of Black cool. It was one way for poor youth to defy the weight and gravity of their social class.

Cultural critic Michael Eric Dyson points to the origin of this inner-city consumer craze: "Madison Avenue sends the message to acquire material goods at any cost, and that chant is piped into Black urban centers where drugs and crime flourish."[3] Dyson asserts, "Black youth learn to want to 'live large,' to emulate capitalism's excesses on their own turf. This force drives some to rob or kill in order to realize their economic goals."[4] The wealth and success of Black athletes, entertainers, and certain successful criminals upped the ante for the average young Black male, who wanted to show the world that he was valuable. Exhibiting the "look" of wealth and power (e.g., gold chains, leather jackets, luxury cars—or anything else the market deemed valuable) was integral.

Nike's greatest success in elevating its shoes to larger-than-life status came with the pairing of Michael Jordan and Spike Lee in the "It's gotta be the shoes!" television and print ad campaign of the late 1980s and early 1990s. In the commercials, directed by Lee, he reprises his ultra-dorky wannabe,

Mars Blackmon, from the 1986 film *She's Gotta Have It*. In the ads, Mars is infatuated with Jordan's superhuman basketball talent and how everything (even women) seems to come to MJ so easily. Unable to fathom that Jordan could achieve that much success based on his own merit or cool, Blackmon draws his own conclusion: "It's gotta be the shoes!"

These commercials garnered street credibility by featuring two prominent and inventive Black males debating the powers of a specific product. The product in these ads alternates between Black-male prowess and the shoes. Jordan epitomizes all that is virtuous in a young Black man, while the scrawny, hyperactive, big-square-glasses-wearing Lee is the antithesis of sex appeal, talent, and cool. He makes unabashed appeals to the camera: "Is it the shoes? Is it the extra-long [Nike] shorts? Come on, money, it's gotta be the shoes!" Cultural historian Paul Gilroy has a more critical reading:

> *[The characters are] revealed as emissaries in a process of cultural colonization, and Mars Blackmon's afterlife as a Nike advertisement is the most insidious result. Through that character above all, Lee set the power of street style and speech to work not just in the service of an imagined racial community but an imaginary Blackness which exists exclusively to further the interests of corporate America.*[5]

As Gilroy charges in his critique, this campaign blatantly displays how black vernacular English (aka Ebonics) and hip-hop signifiers are appropriated in the mainstream marketing of consumer goods. With a hip-hop beat as the soundtrack and Mars Blackmon's B-boy attitude and gold medallion, what Nike is actually selling is thinly veiled. The dorky little thug has all the accoutrements of cool, but he knows he can't really attain authentic coolness (Blackness, in this case) without the symbol of Jordan's power—his shoes. Goldman and Papson find that "it is a strange paradox that the *realer* the talk that is appropriated, the more the act of appropriation ends up romanticizing resistance and turning it into style."[6]

This was the secret to selling cool to Black folks: Impose the dream on the thing and have them continue to strive for it. Impose the image of freedom on the label and have them brand themselves. Cool was sold to me at five years old, at nine, at thirteen, and time and time again through numerous ads, displays, and commercials that reached my peers, too, their bodies branded with labels that seemingly gave them the power of cool.

To my dismay, I found myself more akin to Mars than to MJ. To make matters worse, the red "magic slippers" didn't work for me. I remained earthbound and Air Jordan–less, with no real athletic talent. Not like my cousin Songha; the shoes worked for him. He was a senior, had varsity letters in five sports, was on the honor committee, and led the multicultural forum at our school, Episcopal High School in Alexandria, Virginia, the alma mater of John McCain.

In 1991, I moved from New York City, the epicenter of

racial and cultural mixing, to this all-white-all-boys boarding school steeped in Southern tradition. Confederate flags were common in the dorm rooms as a symbol of "Southern pride." My grades were average, and I couldn't play sports. The only reason I got in was because they thought I would be the next Songha, the epitome of cool. But, after seeing me take a jump shot, basketball star Andre Gilbert looked at me with scorn. "You ain't Juice's cousin!" That was Songha's street name in North Philly. I was blessed with the name Hank—which most often got the response "What kind of name is that for a Black guy?" In other words, Andre made it clear that I had no chance at being cool.

At lunch, all the Black kids would sit together and play the dozens—"joning," as they put it in D.C. "You helmethead motherfucker, you can't say shit"; "Hank, you look like the Black Bart Simpson. Didn't I see you on a T-shirt somewhere?" Typically, I had no comebacks. Songha, on the other hand, was always ready. "Man, look at you jokers," he would say, "looking like a buncha . . . " It didn't matter what he said—nobody could ever really top it. He was the captain of the basketball team but, amazingly, never too cool to hang with anybody. He was as comfortable, confident, and content around the nerds as he was with the boys with Dixie flags and racist tendencies. You could find Songha in their rooms, greeting you with a smile and a wink as they jockeyed for his attention and validation—just like the rest of us.

I was on the other end of the spectrum. I got beat up for challenging a wrestler with Confederate statues in his room. All year long, I rode the bench in football, wrestling, and track. A defining moment was when a white kid named Hunter Brawly gave me a lesson on race in a room full of Black boys. Hunter broke down my lack of cool to its essence: "Man, *I'm* Blacker than you. I can dance better than you, I can play ball better than you . . . as a matter of fact, you don't even talk Black!" I could see by the faces of the other boys in the room that he must have had a point. I was Black in label only.

The next year I transferred to Duke Ellington School for the Arts, a predominantly Black school, and probably one of the coolest places to go to high school. Digable Planets, Stevie Wonder, Jodeci, and Hillary Clinton and the like would pop in regularly for visits. This school was the polar opposite of Episcopal. There was a Black pride assembly virtually every week. The few white, Asian, and Latino kids usually sat there looking a little perplexed.

One thing didn't change, though: I was still an outsider. "Hank! What kind of name is that for a Black person?!⁷ You can't dance! Why you talk that way? You shyyy!"

Things began to turn around for me during my junior year, when a group of us discovered alternative hip-hop groups like the Hieroglyphics and songs like "93 'Til Infinity," by Souls of Mischief. We formed our own crew of "bohemians."

Like sixties funky worms with waves and perms. Just sendin' junky rhythms right down ya block. We be to rap what key be to lock . . . But I'm cool like that . . .

We discovered Digable Planets' *Reachin': A New Refutation*

of Time and Space album (1993), took it literally, and called ourselves Earthbound. We were a consortium of graffiti writers, hip musicians, dancers, and actors led by the few Afrocentric girls in the school. Ironically, we were the only integrated clique at Ellington. At first we were cast off as weirdos, but by graduation we were iconoclasts.

Looking back, I recognize that I learned everything I needed to know about race and cool in those years. I remember that one white kid was treated differently than the others: "Topaz ain't white, he's cool!" He played the saxophone and sported a top hat (no brands), spoke to everybody like a friend, and always had a paper bag of funk tapes in his backseat. Like Songha, he always seemed comfortable in situations where others might have looked or felt out of place. It seemed effortless, authentic.

I began to notice that the coolest kids weren't the ones who could perform Blackness or whiteness the best; they were the ones who could flow seamlessly from metaphorical coast to coast without a ruffle. They weren't changed by situations, labels, or peers; peers, labels—rather, situations—were changed by them. They were adaptable. Songha and so many of my friends revealed in their special ways a message about cool that contradicted what corporate America was selling—that cool comes from within. Although it hadn't hit me yet, the disparity between what the brands were promising me and the gifts these people possessed was deepening greatly.

Topaz and I wound up both going to NYU. I noticed that he and the other white kids from Ellington became even cooler once they were reintegrated into white peer groups.

One night I ran into him and he invited me to a club that I got into solely because of his cachet. I felt awkward because I was wearing overalls and didn't drink or smoke, like everyone else around us did. I complained to him about how I felt. Topaz took a drag from his cigarette, looked me in the eyes, and said, "If you didn't like what you were wearing, why the fuck did you leave the house that way?"

His words hit me like a ton of bricks. He was right. Why *had* I left the house looking like a farmer? The answer was clear as day: because I had felt like it! So why be ashamed? Who cared if people didn't get it? I was still the same guy whom Topaz wanted to kick it with and whom Songha proudly called his little brother. I could flow.

A few months later, Songha revealed his secret for winning people over. We had just glided past the velvet rope at an exclusive club, when I asked him (for the millionth time), "How'd you do it?" He said, "With a wink and a smile." After I prodded him for further explanation, he told me, "They don't know that I only have five dollars in my pocket. It doesn't matter! You see, Hank, I'm the richest poor man alive."

Songha's wealth was in his spirit. He believed in himself, so others did, too. I suppose that's why they called him Juice—his charisma was electric, though he preferred to be called Eclectic. It was 2000, the dawn of the era of bling, but it didn't matter if he had the most material value, because he had an inner confidence that no one could knock down.

Not long after I had this revelation, Songha was murdered while leaving a club in Philadelphia. The killers were robbing Songha's friends for platinum and diamond-encrusted chains. The quest for legitimacy had shifted from acquiring Jordans to getting flashy chains—more valuable than community, more valuable than people's lives, or so it seemed. People wanted more than $150 sneakers. They wanted to be "big pimpin'," with Jay-Z's money. In that materialistic frenzy, a teenage boy told his friends, "I'll be right back, I wanna get a chain." Then, for reasons still unknown, he took the only thing of value on Songha's person that night. Not the silver chain I had brought back to him from Carnival in Trinidad, not the $20 in his pocket—just his soul.

The words of a friend, when he heard the news, still echo in my mind: "The worst part about this is that we don't have to ask if the killers were Black." He turned out to be right (the crew was caught two months later at the same club, after murdering someone else on a quest for a chain). But the question burned in my head: *Why?* Over the years, I've come to understand that there are many reasons, but most of all, the killer didn't have someone like Songha to tell him the secret. Otherwise, he would have better understood the value of soul and not forsaken it for cool.

NOTES

1. Lyrics from the theme song to *Good Times*, the American sitcom that originally aired from February 8, 1974, until August 1, 1979, on the CBS television network.

2. I later found out that the name of my shoes was Nike Cortez, for the conquistador who colonized the inhabitants of Mexico for Spain in the fifteenth century and "discovered" California. I find irony now in this, in light of the strong likelihood that Mexican sweatshop workers manufactured the shoes. But when I was five years old, those things didn't matter much.

3. Michael Eric Dyson. *Between God and Gangsta Rap* (New York: Oxford University Press, 1996), 58.

4. Dyson, 58. Also, Naomi Klein, *No Logo* (New York: Picador, 2002), 76, in which Klein cites a broader trend, " . . . where the hip-hop philosophy of 'living large' saw poor and working-class kids acquiring status in the ghetto by adopting the gear and accoutrements of prohibitively costly leisure activities such as skiing, golfing, even boating . . . Once Tommy was firmly established as a ghetto thing, the real selling could begin—not just to the comparatively small market of poor inner-city youth but to the much larger market of middle-class white and Asian kids who mimic black style in everything from lingo to sports to music. . . Hilfiger's marketing journey feeds off the alienation at the heart of America's race relations: selling white youth on the fetishization of black style, and black youth on their fetishization of white wealth."

5. Paul Gilroy, *Small Acts* (London: Serpents' Tail, 1993).

6. *Nike Culture,* 102.

7. I was always ready with my list of Black Hanks, including baseball player Hank Aaron, college basketball player Hank Gathers, and jazz great Hank Smith, to no avail.

AUTHENTICITY
STACEYANN
CHIN

As a teenager, I never considered myself one of the cool people. At thirteen, I was gawky and prone to having long, confrontational conversations about mitosis and velocity. I also nursed a serious case of acne, which I knew would forever block access to the smooth-faced in crowd at my Catholic, all-girls high school in Montego Bay, Jamaica. Those girls shrieked, and made silly jokes, and followed trends with such ease. They had parents. They did not have unending arguments with boys. I, on the other hand, had no parents, a brutal home life, and the niggling feeling that I was the only person in church who didn't buy the existence of God. I did not fit in anywhere. I longed to be inside the circle of belonging.

At school, I watched those girls, listened to them, trying to figure out what made them so comfortable with each other. At home I mimicked their laughter, their responses to each other, and found that it didn't make me feel good. It made me feel a bit like a liar. The gaggle of giggling girls began to look a little like yellow baby chickens in a coop, and it was hard to tell one chick from the other. I gleaned the message: To be accepted, you had to lose yourself, give yourself away. And that did not feel like a fair exchange to me.

I thought hard about the situation, watched them carefully, and decided I didn't want to be just another clone laughing under the big tree at lunch. If there were trends being followed, I wanted to be one of the girls setting them. It was then that I noticed the attitude of the ringleaders: They weren't nervous about speaking out, and they did not seem worried about what anyone thought when they walked into a room. I saw through the conformity to the confidence that lay beneath, and started acting on my instincts like it was the most normal thing in the world. I experimented with saying whatever came into my head, and found that when I spoke with authority, people took me seriously, no matter what I said. If I acted like I didn't care if they liked me, they liked me even more.

I began to let my individuality shine. I took to wearing odd clothes—a boys' button-down shirt with a comic strip drawn into the fabric, floor-length skirts instead of minis. I began to speak my mind loudly, clearly, and without apology at all times. I started to say what I thought to anyone and everyone—it did not matter to whom. When I had the impulse to mimic everyone else, I acted against it and did the opposite.

The effect was astounding. The other girls did more than tolerate my odd clothing, uncensored utterances, and overuse of multisyllabic words; they looked forward to my outbursts and collapsed into hysterics when I said something irreverent about a nun or a teacher. Many of them, scarcely recovered from belly-bursting squealing, would beg, "Say it again, Staceyann. Please, say it like that again!" I designed a new category of being, an authentic way of moving. I was quirky, crazy, different—just plain Staceyann. And thus began the death of my desire to be anyone else and, I dare say, the birth of what others have come to identify in me as, yes, that's right—cool.

My newfound swagger sustained me through the rest of my troubled teens; it nurtured an unyielding sense of self that served me well when I moved from Montego Bay to attend college in Kingston. I walked how I wanted, talked how I wanted, ate what I wanted, read what I wanted, and eventually dated whomever I wanted—even girls. And when I experienced society's brutal homophobic backlash, that swagger kept me sane and underscored my decision to move away from my home country; I thought it was better to flee than to remain and conform to a heterosexual way of life that rang inauthentic inside me.

When I decided to take my chances with the larger-than-life culture of New York, I worried I might lose this ineffable quality I had cultivated. I didn't quite know how I was going to be lesbian *and* Jamaican. I also feared the effect of the great melting pot; people told me the United States swallowed people whole. I remember making a promise to myself when I landed at JFK on August 20, 1997: never to lose my ability to speak my mind without apology.

When foreigners enter U.S. territory, we are forced to define ourselves, to carve out a new niche for our identity. In the 1960s, Caribbean immigrants were tagged as coconuts. We were the butt of jokes about banana boats and being Uncle Toms. I can't recall how many times I have heard the joke about the hardworking Jamaican with three jobs, or five jobs, or seven jobs—one for every day of the week. Like the girls in school who'd traded their individualism, many immigrants trade out their Jamaican-ness to avoid the hassle. When I arrived in New York and began to meet these folks, they told me that yes, they were Jamaican but hadn't been home in years, or could hardly understand "Jamaicans who talk with that thick Jamaican accent." They told me that though they were born in Jamaica, they had American citizenship now, and no longer saw Jamaica as home.

I did not see them as distinct or fearless; they seemed weaker somehow, like they had lost the very thing that made them powerful. I had worked too hard, dug too deep, to turn back to that sheeplike identity. So I grabbed hold of the undeniable power of self I had carried with me across the sea and boasted the Jamaican-lesbian strut. I wore black, yellow, and gold stripes whenever I could and spoke loudly and frequently about being gay. I wore my Jamaican-ness, my lesbian-ness, my so-called differences, with pride. I remained loud, quick to anger and argument, and just as quick to go wild and laugh uncontainably. I couldn't wait to start "acting Jamaican" when I met a countryman. I needed only to open my mouth, and sure enough, the question came: "Which part of de rock you from?" I relished the twenty-minute conversation about how hard it was to get good Jamaican food, or the last time who went home, or the tragedy of crime on the island, the falling dollar, and, for a while, the miracle of our Jamaican brother Colin Powell.

In public, I reveled in how people responded to my colorful interactions. I found myself using Patois phrases I would never have used in Jamaica. In the States, Jamaican cuss words came easily and frequently to my lips—even though I never cussed in Patois in Jamaica. Along with my Jamaican brethren and sistren, I re-created Jamaica all over this American land. I brought the sound and the rhythm of a lived Jamaica, a utilitarian Jamaica, to places where we traditionally existed only within the subcategory of reggae music. I made myself visible; I owned my undebatable, singular, Black, Jamaican, lesbian, poet self. My vow served me well: Within American borders, I felt my cool differently—it was in my accent and my pride. My refusal to assimilate kept me stable—and, like in high school, it continued to magnetize. Readers, editors, audience members all responded to what Grace Jones called her Jamaican Guy, and to what I can describe only as my Jamaican Cool.

Young poets now tell me that they want to write like me, to read their poems like me. They want me to give them the how-to. And, sad to say, I'm not sure how to do that. I don't know how much is content, how much is diction, and how much of it is just the way I deliver my words, the way I use my body onstage. Initially, I simply wanted to vent my personal feelings, to carve a space in which to let my Stacey-ann live. I read my first poem at the Nuyorican Poets Cafe. At the time I didn't know I was doing anything radical. I was just being myself.

I sat for hours listening to people reading stories about where they were from, the struggles they were experiencing around being Black, or Korean American, or Cherokee American. Poets shared intimate, angry, funny poems about their sex lives, their cities—Kansas City, Detroit, Honolulu. Those poems ran the gamut of suffering and loss and longing and triumph, and made me feel like my words, however different, however controversial, had a place in the room. I added my name to the open-mic list and read a journal entry about being from Jamaica, about being a lesbian. I described the things I missed, about the language I missed speaking. I remember the hush in the room when I compared the flesh of a Jamaican mango to the flesh of a Jamaican woman; how not being able to eat that mango rendered me a divided self. I lashed out at the homophobia that drove me from my home. It felt good cussing out Jamaica with her own tongue. It gave me room to quarrel with my country without relinquishing my cultural identity. The more I shouted in my own voice about my own experience, the more Jamaican I felt and the more authentic my voice became.

I began to read the work of other women who were from the Caribbean. On the page, I did not have access to their voices, but I had access to their line breaks. June Jordan's work challenged me to speak about more than my personal tragedies. Audre Lorde's essays about cancer incited me to take up the issue of health insurance as a right. Alice Walker's *The Color Purple* showed me that incest didn't happen just in poor Jamaican homes. I kept performing, and when I came out onstage barefoot and Afro'd, speaking with my unmistakably Jamaican accent, audiences became more attentive.

I invoked the span of my social trajectory from the easy feel of the rural one-room shack to the tourist capital of Kingston, where the gulf between the wealthy and those who lived far below any measurable poverty line was kept from the eyes of paying guests. I conjured the cramped tenement yards, the daily squabbles, and the surprisingly human philosophies that charted the lives of those who could not afford large, safe rooms of their own.

When I put to words the breadth of my Jamaican experience—the poetry, music, yawps, funeral wails, clipped logic of the educated, resigned laughter of the poor, and myriad places where everything meets and becomes one giant front yard—my voice rang out guttural, my pauses unmistakably a product of that complicated yard. I wrote my truth, and it wasn't Bob Marley's. I wrote the middle class, the church-going grandmother, the present-day Jamaican American immigrant, into my poems. I talked about the schizophrenic journey from poor, abandoned, biracial child to college-educated, lesbian poet-philosopher living in Brooklyn, New York. I intended to break the old Jamaican mold by being an unabashedly Jamaican woman who reveled in falling in love with other women.

I expected to face some resistance, but by the time I announced I was a lesbian my audiences were completely mine, and I theirs. And so I was unprepared for the rush of appreciation that came, not only from Jamaicans living in New York City, but also from Americans all across the country, and eventually from Danes, South Africans, and Australians. At first, no one talked about the content of my work; the blatant sexual and blasphemous references were largely ignored. Instead I received compliments about my diction and my clever use of language. People said they experienced the poems I performed like jazz. There was something African in them, decidedly primal, they said. What I heard when they called my performances "unique" was an affirmation of the power of speaking in your own language, and being unafraid to say out loud what you know to be true.

As I get older, I find I am less vigilant against departures from the way I speak. I have moments where I catch a word coming out of my mouth sounding Brooklynite. I wonder how the next decade, or the next two decades, will alter my delivery, my rhythm, my Afro-Jamerican jazz. I question if I will become less valuable as I begin to read my poems quietly onstage.

But mostly I don't worry about it. I try to be grateful for this identity that allows my politics, my experiences, to be seen. Most days, I feel so lucky to be able to do what I love, to love what I do. For me, every performance is an exhalation. Every poem requires a letting go of the lips, a release of the breath, a push of sound designed to shatter the boundaries between what I am, what people perceive me to be, and what I really, really wish I could be. It's a delicate dance—this mad dash through art and artifice and actuality.

I may never know the real value of these public, staccato confessions. There is no way to measure how great the impact is, or how many people remain changed or affected by them after I leave. I only know that to be me, to remain true to that self I adore, I must say my truth out loud. If I don't I will be someone else. And it has been forever since I have wanted to be that. I have my own cool now.

THE SCREAM
ULLI
K.
RYDER

I come from a family of nonscreamers. That doesn't mean they didn't fight against injustice, didn't get angry, didn't hate some of the things this country has done and continues to do. But they didn't scream. They marched and sat in and drew on Christian love and forgiveness, and made protest art so beautiful some people might miss the protest. But they didn't raise their voices. They didn't rail against the machine. They left that to me.

I was born Black. Or so I've been told. My mother, descendant of Swiss immigrants, explained to me that when she married my father she understood she would be having Black children. It was 1967 and there wasn't another choice. The rule of hypodescent meant that I was Black, no matter who my mother was. Just like my father—descendant of Africans, Native Americans, and Europeans—knew he was Black when he was a child. It was 1937. There wasn't another choice. But then there was me. Born Black but with this white mother and this light skin and this childhood that did not contain many other Black children. There were Brooke and her brother Cesar, adopted by our (white) neighbors. There were what I thought of as the "real" Black kids in my grade school—Buddy and Tyrone and Cherry and Michael.

I guess my father was cool, but he was my father and so, really, how cool could he have been? He was an artist, which made him kind of cool. My mother was decidedly uncool. It was the 1970s and she did macramé and watercolors and meditated. I was certain that the parents of Buddy or Tyrone or Cherry or Michael did not macramé or meditate. I didn't know what they did do, but I was sure it wasn't any of those things. They certainly didn't live on a Buddhist commune like the one where my mother and I took up residence after she and my father divorced.

I was Black there because no one else was. There were Germans and Koreans and French and Cambodians and Poles and plain old American white folks but no one like me. So I got to be the special Black girl. Maybe not cool, but special. That was something. I put on my little gray robe and sometimes got to ring the big bell that called everyone to the Dharma Room. On Saturdays I climbed on the high altar and polished the Buddha, taking great care between the folds of his robe and polishing each golden fingernail till it gleamed. I spoke to him in whispers so no one else could hear. We understood each other, that Buddha and I. He was the only gold one and I was the only Black one and we both spent a long time watching others when they thought we weren't paying attention.

My mom and I spent about eight years in the Buddhist commune, until I was fifteen years old. Almost immediately, music—and the wider world generally—became more important than my secrets with Buddha.

As with most teens, my introduction to music was through my friends. Because I listened to what they listened to, I missed the rap phenomenon and sidestepped hip-hop, but those Black punks got me. Their dissatisfaction and dis-ease. The dissonance and discord in their music. Their ability to say what, precisely and exactly, was on their minds. Like white punks, they called bullshit. Unlike (most) white punks, they called bullshit on whiteness. H.R. and Bad Brains, 24-7 Spyz, Fishbone—all flailing arms and legs, flailing braids and dreads. Screaming injustice, screaming love, screaming, "I see all your hypocrisy and I will not be part of it!"

I had never seen Black people just let it all out like that. My father's response to crushing racism was to be as perfect as possible. He ironed his jeans, wore expensive suits, and was never once seen eating watermelon (not even in the privacy of his own home). But here were H.R. and the Black punks: ripped clothing, kind of dirty, screaming and rolling around on the floor. Having convulsions from trying to make us all hear, to understand, that Black pain and Black rage. It was like watching freedom.

Punk had, till then, always seemed a white thing. All-white audiences. All-white bands. The only exception was

The Clash. They weren't Black, but something about four working-class white Brits hit me. They were disaffected youth, yes, but so were Murphy's Law and The Cro-Mags and Sick of It All. But The Clash had smarts and the knowledge that wider forces in the world made them poor and kept folks like them poor; and they made the racial connection, which hooked me for real: "White riot—I wanna riot / White riot—a riot of my own / Black people got a lot of problems / but they don't mind throwing a brick / White people go to school / where they teach you how to be thick." It was the mid-eighties and I had no hope of seeing The Clash play live, but in my room Joe Strummer spoke to me like I spoke to the Buddha. Underneath the lyrics, another sound, telling me someone else out there might just understand.

And I did get to see H.R., throwing his body on the ground, literally screaming lyrics from every cell: "In this house of suffering / I got to let some joy in / I hear freedom will win / where oh where can Jah love be now / it's here in the hearts of your own children." At a time when I fit in nowhere, when I was taken over by the usual teenage angst plus a racial ambiguity that discomfited, here was a way out. White punk rock was dominated by the teenage-angst aspect, but Black punks used the white British invention to say, *I hate whiteness and the oppression and pain it is causing me.* It was appropriation, though I didn't know the word at the time. But this time, the Black guys were outpunking the white punks: H.R.'s bullet-train-speed lyrics, the growl that almost, *almost* made his words unintelligible.

But what got me most was that, instead of worrying over being outsiders, instead of holding on to all the racism, the kicks and jabs, the Black punks said, *Screw you—you want me outside? I'm gonna go so far outside, you won't know what to do with me. I'll be so far out, I'll be in.* And then, suddenly, whether I was Black or not or cool or not didn't even matter. For the first time, through those songs, I felt that someone understood that I wasn't just another angry, disconnected teenager, but that so much of that was rooted in race and living in a racist society. I no longer had to fight that battle alone.

And those Black punks knew their past; musical traditions like jazz and blues and reggae filled the gaps and spaces between the thrashing and wailing. Beneath the surface, sometimes exploding up and out, was this white-hot heat of generations that made them like nothing I'd ever heard before. I would sit on the side of the stage and just let the music pound into me, vibrating all my muscles and organs, not minding the sweat or spit flying from the singers. I would look out into the audience and see those few other Black punks in a churning sea of whites, all having the same religious experience as I was, moshing and swaying to the subterranean rhythms below the bass line.

Years later I heard Dizzy Gillespie talk about the innovation of bebop. He said they played so many notes so fast, the white jazz guys couldn't keep up. The Black musicians had taken back the form that had been taken from them. Black punk was kind of like that: altering the form to make it theirs. Appropriation, reappropriation, innovation, evolution. The epitome of Black cool. They give us Christianity and Jesus, and we make sorrow songs and spirituals to guide each other out of bondage. Give us white British Empire punk rock and we turn it around: Slavery and domination are your original sins and the slaves are rising up. Watch out.

I'm no longer sure that I'm Black and I'm no longer sure that it matters. Perhaps Black cool is not just Black bodies but all the things those bodies and minds and hearts do and feel and express. We have entered what is being called the multi-racial millennium. I have a choice that I didn't have as a child and that my father never had. I can be multiracial. I can be multiracial every day. Or just on some days. Or just in front of some people. Or never.

Where is Black cool in the multiracial millennium, when Beyoncé looks like J.Lo looks like Britney Spears? Same hair, same tan, same choreography. Hybrid hotties and beige beauties. It's all so . . . flat and pretty and airbrushed. Where is the screaming? If Black cool grows out of Black rage and Black survival, what happens in a supposedly post–civil rights, postrace, color-blind world?

But maybe I'm getting ahead of myself with that kind of talk. Isn't there still plenty to scream about? Black women are demonized for (allegedly) not protecting their children, even in the womb. Black men in Angola, in Folsom, in prisons everywhere, on death row and in solitary confinement, might tell us Black struggle is a constant struggle. Freedom is not ours yet. Color-blind might be the new Jim Crow. Just ask James Anderson. If you could. If he hadn't been beaten to death and run over for sport by angry, bored white teenagers.

Black punk—all punk—is still around. Some of the same bands still play. The Clash are long gone and Joe Strummer is dead, but Bad Brains still tour. Fishbone are seemingly always on tour—eclipsed by white punk-inspired bands in the SoCal scene, like the Red Hot Chili Peppers and No Doubt, and Green Day in San Francisco.

I haven't kept up with the newer bands. I like my oldies. They're the ones who saved me in the first place. And I have less need for saving now. Less need for the family and community punk provides. Although the general consensus is that once a punk, always a punk. The Clash are playing on my stereo right now. I have all their records (yes, records—black vinyl). Some days only "Pressure Drop" will do. Some days I'm still that fifteen-year-old punk. I still scream. I look around at what we continue to do to each other, and the only answer is to scream.

I don't see the need to scream disappearing anytime soon. In ten years, fifty years, one hundred years, I hope kids still listen to Bad Brains and The Clash and Fishbone. For some of them, surviving those teenage years will depend on hearing Black rage unrestrained. Black punk offers a hardcore mix of love and anger and hope and *screw you* and *maybe life sucks today but we don't have to take it suffering in silence*.

Scream, kids, scream!

SOURCES

The Clash, *White Riot*, 1977. Retrieved from www. sing365.com /music/lyric.nsf/White-Riot-lyrics-The-Clash/476228A103 D20262482568AB00325394.

The *Root*. "New York Latest Target of Black Anti-abortion Billboards," February 24, 2011. Retrieved from http://www.theroot.com/views/re-ppnyc-statement-abortion-billboard-targeting-african-americans-nyc.

EVOLUTION

MILES
MARSHALL
LEWIS

What's in a name? Eight months after the release of Miles Davis's controversial, spellbinding fusion album *Bitches Brew*, Dad identified his firstborn as Miles. That early December morning, three months to the day after James Marshall Hendrix asphyxiated on his own vomit, my parents decided on Miles Marshall. But growing up named after those icons, I never felt burdened with trying to measure up to them on any kind of musical level. (Thank God.) If anything, my namesakes held a different kind of crown over my head for me to sport cocked to the side: the crown of cool.

No jazzman was ever a bigger rock star than Miles Davis. The so-called Prince of Darkness went so far beyond categorization that his inspiration for records like *On the Corner* came from funk innovator Sly Stone *and* experimental German composer Karlheinz Stockhausen. Miles set off the whole cool school of jazz with *Birth of the Cool* in the 1950s, but that's not why he built a rep as the genre's coolest player. Miles was cool because he stayed rooted in the now and never looked back; because he knew in his blood that constant evolution causes expansion. Turning down gigs at Fifty-second Street nightclubs like Birdland and opting instead to play the Isle of Wight rock festival for over six hundred thousand fans at a time, he refused to be boxed in.

No rock star was a bigger jazzman than Jimi Hendrix: jam-crazy, improvisational, slavishly devoted to his instrument. In the young rock culture of the 1960s, he demanded the space to be multidimensional in a milieu where no other singer-songwriter looked or sounded anything like him. Hendrix tunes like "The Wind Cries Mary" were lyrically on par with the best of poetic wordsmiths like Bob Dylan or John Lennon. From the moment Hendrix crashed the scene, his brilliant innovations with guitar-amp feedback, along with literally incendiary performance theatrics and an eclectic fashion sense, immediately marked him as a man apart. In an era when Motown's finest were suiting up for the acceptance of mainstream America, Hendrix's rebel tendencies made anticonformity cool for African Americans. (Sporting a Hendrix T-shirt *still* means something well into the twenty-first century, especially if you're of color.)

Miles Davis was the coolest godfather I never had. He launched my writing career: The first thing I ever published, outside of childhood letters to Marvel Comics, was his obituary in my college paper. The first vinyl I spent my own money on was *My Funny Valentine*, his 1964 concert album. Before I turned twenty I'd already seen him play live, twice. When I was a teenager, appreciating all the romance and vulnerability, the solitude and beauty, in the phrasing of Miles's baroque ballads was its own reward. But learning about Miles the man was a separately edifying head trip.

The only autographed anything in our Bronx apartment was a menu from the Greenwich Village jazz club the Bottom Line, Miles's signature snaking down the side. (My father approached him at the bar after a show.) On weekend trips down to the comics shop Forbidden Planet, Pops sometimes cut through the Upper West Side by Miles's place—312 West Seventy-seventh Street—to catch a glimpse of the man or his canary yellow Ferrari Testarossa. My dad and I never spotted it, but I knew he drove one.

In those dawning days of the music video, I watched Miles on TV, decked out colorfully in the hip threads of Yohji Yamamoto and Issey Miyake, wraparound shades in place. Fresh from my first read of Malcolm X's autobiography, I was also impressed by Miles's nationalistic agitprop. (When I was fourteen, Davis told *Jet* magazine, "If somebody told me I had only one hour to live, I'd spend it choking a white man.")

The sports car, the raspy voice, the cool clothes, the militant stance . . . I was impressed by it all. Miles Davis was my first exposure to an African American Renaissance man, and all the things I thought made him great influenced what I aspired to become. I am as devoted to hiphop culture now as Miles was to jazz, judging by his 1990 autobiography. His late-'40s dalliance with French chanteuse Juliette Gréco was semiscandalous for the pre–civil rights era; I've been living in Paris for the past seven years, married to my French *choubidou*, Christine. And I've made my share of race-man choices— graduating from a historically Black college; writing and editing at *XXL*, *Vibe*, and BET, all bastions of Black culture.

The same evolutionary spirit Jay-Z details in "On to the Next One" defined Miles Davis's attitude for over four decades. By the time *Birth of the Cool* spawned a whole new subgenre of jazz in the fifties (typified by light tones and relaxed tempos), Miles was already at the center of the hard-bop scene with records like *Walkin'* (1954). His exploration of musical modes instead of chord progressions blossomed on *Kind of Blue* (1959)— the greatest-selling jazz record of all time—but the about-facing *Sketches of Spain* (1960) followed less than a year later. Inspired by classical and big-band music, it's the most celebrated of his collaborations with arranger Gil Evans. Still, those eleven years of changing the face of music weren't enough.

After a series of feted freebop recordings, Davis dropped his first full-on electric album, *In a Silent Way* (1969), and jazz was never the same. Again. With producer Teo Macero slicing and dicing different takes like a pre-hiphop mixmaster, the jazz-fusion highball *Bitches Brew* (1970) proved there was never any turning back with Miles. Dividing fans and critics alike, *Bitches Brew* made it plain that Miles Davis was always going to do whatever the fuck he wanted. Full of electric guitar and synthesizers, ambient mood and rock-style improvisation, Davis's double album marked the final major stylistic shift in jazz to date. On his final studio album, Miles teamed with producer Easy Mo Bee (future collaborator with rapper Biggie Smalls) and came up with the 1992 Grammy-winning *Doo-Bop* (though I always preferred its more provocative working title, *Blow*). And if you can stay that perpetually innovative while sporting unstructured blazers, nattily tailored suits, snakeskin pants, or buckskin-fringe vests, more power to you.

Miles and his astrological brother-in-arms, Prince—the two Geminis had a mutual admiration—both had an impact on me in my teenage wonder years as eclectic champions of reinvention and ever-reaching development. With Miles, becoming stale, repetitive, or stagnant (creatively or intellectually) was entirely verboten, an invaluably cool lesson to learn at a young age.

There was a time when being Black and loving Jimi Hendrix was like being Black and loving hockey or country music: a curious sort of pursuit for somebody blessed with melanin. Way back when there were few clearer signs of being Black on the outside and white on the inside (the classic old stigma of the "Oreo" African American) than declaring love for James Marshall Hendrix. Yet when it comes to evolving the Black identity, rock music's number one guitar god represents on many levels.

If you have parents who have repeatedly trotted out a dozen familiar stories throughout your life, you know what it felt like to hear—over and over—that my pops had attended the New Year's Eve show Hendrix recorded live for his *Band of Gypsys* album in 1969. (Mom's familiar story is about how our aquarium's fish always swam in waves with "1983 . . . (A Merman I Should Turn to Be)" on the stereo.) In the mix-tape age of my high-school days, Maxell cassettes often streamed favorite Hendrix hits over my Walkman: "If 6 Was 9," "Manic Depression," "Voodoo Child (Slight Return)." In the eighties, *Rolling Stone* reported that Prince had covered "Red House" live somewhere in Europe, and I spent months dissecting different versions of the Hendrix original. Then I got almost ten years' wear out of a vintage, Hendrix-ian suede vest I unearthed at Cheap Jack's, a secondhand shop on Broadway that was anything but cheap.

Plus, we're both Sagittarians.

But one of the coolest things about Jimi Hendrix is how he reframed racial identity by pushing the boundaries of what it meant to be Black. Decades before the eighties' Afropunk movement, Black folks would generally give you a pass for digging on *Band of Gypsys* (recorded with African American bassist Billy Cox and Black drummer Buddy Miles) but roast you alive for appreciating the earlier Jimi Hendrix Experience albums (recorded with his original British bandmates). Black Panthers gave Hendrix heat for conking his hair, idolizing Bob Dylan and the Beatles, and supposedly straying from his musical roots on the chitlin circuit with Little Richard, the Isley Brothers, and others. None of this stopped him from mastering rock and adding to its canon with widely influential work like *Electric Ladyland*.

Hendrix was Hendrix, unconcerned with staying true to anyone's ideas of Blackness but his own. He outplayed Eric Clapton, totally wrested Dylan's "All Along the Watchtower" from the rock poet's hands, and indiscriminately jammed with everyone from Cream and Steve Winwood to Billy Preston and Stevie Wonder. A master of the blues by way of Jupiter, Hendrix took the Black-rooted music form halfway across the universe and back, expanding its possibilities in ways immediately exploited by Led Zeppelin, Funkadelic, Black Sabbath, and scores of others.

I discovered our shared middle name reading a Hendrix biography in college. Pops let me discover that one on my own, saying that if I felt connected to my namesake, then I'd find out eventually—by which time I trailed my red clay-soiled campus in combat boots, silver ring through my nose, a tattoo freshly inked on my deltoid (all pretty rare at Black universities in 1990). From the vantage of 1990, Hendrix revealed ways of being Black that went far beyond the then-modern models of Bobby Brown or Ice Cube. Waving his own freak flag, breaking away from a Black image that whites might've felt more comfortable with, Hendrix rather single-handedly evolved Black style for all the Lenny Kravitzes, Jean-Michel Basquiats, and TV on the Radios to follow.

My favorite Miles Davis tune of all time is "Générique." My all-time favorite Jimi Hendrix song is "Third Stone from the Sun." And my favorite lesson learned from both my namesakes is—to paraphrase rapper Rakim—that constant evolution causes expansion. Break beyond boundaries of the tried and true, and therein lies the mother lode.

THE POSSE
ESTHER
ARMAH

Driving on that mad dusty road from Accra to Kumasi on my
way to my mama's village. Akumadan. It had been too long.
I was at home—one of them, anyway—in Ghana. *Driving* is
a generous word for what dude at the wheel was doing. That
road is a roller-coaster adventure, its existence evidence of
the country's political progress, its condition proof of a serious lack of attention. Damn, I turned my head away from
what kind of driving is that, dude? and watched the grace of
women in cloth, balancing bounty on heads while watching children move through the dust and heat. Watched men
toting lumber, in fields taking care of business. Never tired
of watching this grace and focus in action. We got to the village. Eventually.

Sitting in village life for me is like catching up with dear
old friends with whom time hasn't really moved much and it
feels like you only saw them yesterday. Comforting familiar.
Watching children move together, check each other, play

together; smiling as women gather in care of themselves and their community.

My aunt called me over. I knew that call. I squatted down next to her. I can still see her eyes: chocolate, smiling, a little wicked—eyes that always meant trouble. She tightened her cloth around her waist. Started with pleasantries. How's New York? New home's cool. How was it treating my spirit? I've another home, a belonging space. She smiled at me. I smiled back. I waited. She let me wait. She was pounding *gari*, making one of my favorites. I could smell the pepper. For that tastiness, known to no other space but this village and my Mama's people, I would sit and wait.

The question came. Are you dating? I smiled back at her. Hope to. She continued to pound. Smiled at me again, reached over and hugged me and spoke ancient words in my ear. Don't forget to just sit in his spirit, take time and see how that feels; it might fit yours, it might not. You won't know unless you just sit with the spirit of him, not necessarily in conversation but keeping company with his thoughts.

Ever sat in the spirit of someone else? Just sat, felt their spirit, the quiet of them, their emotionality, their whole self— ever done that? It can be scary, feeling that emotional vulnerability. Like falling, and yet you have wings—just takes a minute to discover then feel them. It is that wisdom I love, cherish, and own about the together that is the cool of the collective of village life. We know how to sit still with another's spirit. To be alone, and together.

I'm a diaspora chick, so my Blackness spans galaxies known and unknown, Octavia Butler style, Toni Morrison flavored. It's a beloved kindred thing that has so many more than nine lives, but no shelf life. Born in London to mom and pop birthed in Ghana, I have a traveler's spirit that has seen, made homes in, created communities out of, and worked on three continents—Europe, Africa, America—and so have been blessed to tune in to visions and versions of Blackness that excited, delighted, disappointed, devastated, intimidated, and impressed. Mine is an ancient modern freshness with evolving swag. And right now I can tell you from experience, in the age of Obama and beyond, the collective, the posse, the ability to sit with one another's spirit in the dark, ain't just cool, it's crucial.

Why now? Legacy. I'm a movement, baby—we all are. Global Blackness or African American, we're the beneficiaries, inheritors, products of movements that changed nations, shifted the direction of countries bent on injustice toward this melanin fabulousness. My pop was a movement man. He, in 1957—like me in 2008—cried as he witnessed the election of the first Black president. For him it was Kwame Nkrumah in Ghana; for me it was Barack Obama. But the fight to get to that moment took its toll.

From the brutality of slavery and the abolitionist movement to the shackles of Jim Crow segregation and then the Civil Rights movement, the boldness and bigness of collective Blackness was an unstoppable machine that chugged its way from protests on the street to creating legislation to finally recognizing humanity while being consistently assaulted by all these forces. At first the fight was for presence—literally, to be alive, to stay that way—then it was to be in places where whiteness reigned. We caught hell. We got hurt. We bled. We got up. We fell down. We got up again. We scored victories. We lost loved ones. We sustained wounds and scars. We died. Living those battles, who has time to tend to all the wounds sustained—seen and unseen—while fighting to breathe?

We built up our resistance, became part of a resistance movement and wore that *R* on our chests like a badge of honor. We worked for it, earned it, deserved it, flaunted that sucker. Struggle was our lover; it was this intimate place of living, breathing being. Resistance—the act or power of resisting, opposing, withstanding, was a calling for Blackness, and evidence of this extraordinary strength. We've done that for a long, long time. And we have wounds. Where are yours? Did they heal? Or did the scars and the skin and your soul keloid?

How does the resistance we so needed then really work for you, me, us now? How does its legacy shape how we move through our worlds and deal with those we love? Has that resistance, that struggle, been our lover for too long? And what would it mean to break up? What would it mean to break down some of the walls we've built around ourselves for survival? What would it mean to reconnect, to really "roll with our peeps"? To sit in silence, together, the ultimate posse?

Some cultural critics and writers say our generation is disconnected from that trauma. I hear that. I put it this way: All the trauma sustained wasn't treated. That's like telling a driver in the middle of a crash, the car somersaulting through the air, that he's supposed to check what's happening with the cars behind and in front of him and then operate on himself at the same time. Who does that? No one. So we grabbed a Band-Aid, bandage, rag, whatever, to cover the wounds we could see, to make sure we didn't bleed to death. Some did; the rest made do. But those wounds and scars passed from generation to generation, emotionally. Affecting how we move through the world, deal with and relate to one another; how we construct our institutions—not brick-and-mortar ones, but selves, each other, families, community. It's time to heal that part of ourselves. I call this emotional justice, and I say the collective is crucial for this "emotional justice" movement.

It's time to look deeper at the cool of the crew and draw on its roots: the strength of the village. Because here we are: bold, brilliant, badass, brutal. The bandages came off a while back. They've been gone for a minute. Our progress is now defined by even more than our presence. Occupying seats of power, splashing the phenomenon of hip-hop across the globe; from hood to Harvard to the White House, the brilliance of Blackness keeps evolving. It's like we built this matrix of impossibility and then moved our asses in. But now it's trickier: The wounds in the souls of Black folk are now shielded by such flyness, they often cannot even be seen. That untreated trauma was born with us and it stayed as we grew.

To heal, we need each other. As a people of movements, we aren't unfamiliar with rolling with our crew, but I'm talking about being together for our emotional selves. I'm talking about emotional spaces: cultivating connections, creating global caramel-chocolate fusions with bridge-building modern tools, like social media, and more traditional ones, like live gatherings in conversation, to hear and talk tough, difficult, transformative truths. I'm talking about navigating emotional battlegrounds armed with the flyest weapon and shield—us, not me or I—but *us*. I'm talking about created corners where we find more than sanctuary and soothing. I'm talking about something ancient and futuristic. I'm talking about the cool of the collective.

Don't get me wrong, I ain't talkin' Hollyweird Blackness. Our togetherness is not this romantic, rose-colored, fairy-dust, disappear-in-a-mist kinda thing—it is way more special than that. And I am not talking about an intellectual space, either—as sexy as the brain is, that is not what I mean. Emotional justice can't be about theory, philosophy, or analysis. It comes from back-in-the-day ways, all intercontinental and married with modern–ish. A part of me is straight up out of the village. I also now live in the murder capital, where they murder for capital and possible innocence is no deterrent to execution, so executing togetherness is a careful craft. But Mama is an Ashanti lady, raised in the villages of Ghana's Kumasi. Pop, too—different village, his childhood spot, Anochie. And it's the memory of them gathering and being gathered that brings its own deliciousness. It reps spaces and moments that reveal the freshness of together in culture, color, language, flavor, that doesn't necessarily deny or demand you abandon individualism.

Traditional gatherings of comfort for Black folk have been places of worship, where collective voices raised in prayer or song bring their own spiritual nourishment. But the church is sometimes without sanctuary for our bruised souls. Too often it is a safe house only to those covered by fly Sunday threads. It is not home, nor is it a safe space for the toughest truths. Rolling with our people in church, many of us have felt its power but also its restriction. The trouble is that individualism grew out of that experience of alienation and became the new religion. We started to worship at the altar of being apart. Our new mantra was Self all day. This growing obsession with individualism has caused confusion in the blessing that is solitude, and turned togetherness into a shackle from which to be freed. We got that *ish* wrong.

Our healing need not be this imposed methodology that is a couch, a separate individual, an office with diplomas on a wall. Black healing is not about saviors, gurus, or leaders in the traditional sense of the self-help industry. Therapy is powerful. No doubt. And it works for so, so many. But it is also not our only option, and for some Black folk, it isn't even an option at all. But, I've learned through the panels I created in Manhattan, sometimes togetherness is.

The "Afrolicious: The Emotional Justice Arts and Conversation" series is a space I created using the history I know, the culture I come from, and the reality I live. I wanted to create a place, an energy, a chance to talk about the things we may discuss in private, but keep to ourselves when we're in a room with others. I wanted to explore traditionally defined social-justice issues like incarceration and masculinity in a different way, without analysis and philosophy. I'm talking not about a negation of intellect, but an affirmation of emotionality. Intellect can take you a long way, it may even save your life, but it's our emotionality that keeps interrupting our growth, disrupting progress and motion, and interfering with all manner of evolution. What we need now requires a different energy. Our intellect won't save us—we need emotional calm. Wellness. For so many of us, our emotional bodies are tattered, battered, bruised, untended, neglected, even as we've crafted and entered spaces where our brilliance shines.

In conversation—that is where we need to be, not at a lecture or a learning. Part of this togetherness is feeling another person's spirit through their story, sitting in their emotionality and feeling our way around that. "Afrolicious" is about exchange. When panelists like academic and activist Marc Lamont Hill, academic and author Mark Anthony Neal, and filmmaker Byron Hurt talk about Black Male Privilege in a way that prompts brothers to identify that privilege in their own worlds, that's the cool of the collective. When Jamaican-born poet and writer Staceyann Chin; academic, journalist, and author Doctor Stacey Patton; writer and activist asha bandele; and entrepreneur Dian Brooks talk about the lessons and legacies passed from mother to daughter and provoke conversation about how to draw a line under destructive, but unexamined, emotional legacies, that's the cool of the collective. When author and former social worker Terrie Williams and holistic chef Nathalie Thandiwe talk about how we use food as our comfort and sanctuary even though our bodies are crying out for something else, that, too, rolls out to create the cool of the collective.

Some admit—especially when a sister talks about doing a panel on Black Male Privilege—that they came ready to throw down. But I'm a bridge builder. I look at where global Blackness meets your Blackness, and then find ways to build. I try to create a space without the sensationalist provocation we see in today's reality TV. A safe space where academics talk from their hearts and not their heads to create a different conversation, a different outcome, and a special audience. I'm about seeing how far this emotionality and its power can go, take us, move us. How can we do that in this collective and keep it fresh, preserve its sexy, honor its cool? I may host, create, research, and moderate the programs, but I take notes, too.

I remember when I was a girlchild, my friend's mama would comment on how much time I spent by myself. My daddy—a beautiful, complicated man who rocked three-piece suits and a tie just to go to the corner store—told her I wasn't lonely, just keeping company with my thoughts. That interpretation made my heart smile. That's solitude, keeping company with the first institution—that of self. Hanging out with your own spirit. But hanging out with your spirit is not the same as an obsession with individualism. That obsession can be a cancer to Blackness—not because self ain't fly, too, but because the beauty of together is a forgotten magic we can't afford to lose.

Emotional justice is our next movement; it is this generation's work. Let's create it, explore it, lean on it, turn to it, make use of it. Let's walk with one another. Let's sit quietly in the dark.

SWAGGER
DAWOUD
BEY

Harlem. Late afternoon, 1978. Fifth Avenue between 126th and 127th streets. A woman stands alone, serenely inhabiting the patch of sidewalk on which she stands. Perhaps she's waiting for someone. Or perhaps she's just waiting, resting at the end of the day before heading upstairs to prepare dinner for the people she loves. Or maybe there is no one, and she is simply collecting her thoughts. I can tell from the comfortable way she holds on to the iron fence that she knows this place well. For that moment, she owns that piece of concrete land. It is hers.

I see her one afternoon as I walk the streets of Harlem, looking for people and moments that exemplify this Black metropolis, this place that looms so large in the cultural imagination. I am attempting to make photographs that adequately inscribe, visually, the complexity of a people and a place. I am looking at the ways in which the past and present of Harlem bump up against each other, since all places are both the places they were and the places they are now. I am attracted by the light as much as I am by the woman herself, standing in the light even as the darkness looms around and behind her—she, so deep in thought.

I stand quietly and unobtrusively a few feet away from her and expose two frames of film, but I sense the photograph—indeed, the moment—needs something more, both to layer the pictorial narrative and to give the picture that is building a more complex sense of form. I look down the block to see who might be approaching, what elements I might be able to work into this picture that I am imagining, without knowing exactly what I am waiting for—only that I am waiting for something.

I see two young boys approaching, engaged animatedly in conversation, seemingly oblivious to the rest of the world. I know that if I take a step back, they will pass in front of me and also in front of the woman; they will inhabit the space in between the two of us. As they enter the frame, their gestures mirror each other; their stride is animated, exuberant, and confident. Their beings are full of a youthful bravado evident in their every move. They, too, now own this patch of sidewalk.

They are full of swagger. They are full of cool.

I take the picture, but cannot help thinking: When is swagger real and when is it perceived? Is Black swagger actually confidence and self-command going by a more loaded, and perhaps insidious, name? You know, a kind of cool surrogate of the less appealing "uppity"?

What happens to Black boys with too much swagger? Emmett Till is not here to answer on his own behalf. Visiting Mississippi from his home in Chicago one summer in 1955, the fourteen-year-old Till allegedly whistled at a white woman and was brutally murdered by several white men and thrown into the Tallahatchie River in Mississippi for his supposed transgression. Those folks who snuffed out his young Black life must have thought he was one seriously uppity little Negro. His swagger proved fatal.

swag · ger/ˈswagər/

Verb: Walk or behave in a very confident and typically arrogant or aggressive way: "he swaggered along the corridor."

Noun: A very confident and typically arrogant or aggressive gait or manner.

When I was a young boy, growing up in the Black middle-class neighborhood of St. Albans, in Queens, New York, my mother used to make an example of my friend Michael's older brother. He walked down the street with an exaggerated dip to his step, outfitted with a do-rag that held his processed "conk" in place. My mother would point him out derisively each time he passed our window. "Look at him," she would say, shaking her head. She left no doubt in my mind that whatever Michael's brother *was*, my brother Ken and I had better not even *think* about emulating or becoming it. She equated his swagger with a lack of substance masquerading as bravado. His swagger, which I did not then have a word for, she deemed arrogant, maybe even aggressive. Perhaps even dangerous.

Because the leap from "confident" to "aggressive" is perilously short. And aggressive people are threatening, right? So Black boys and men who carry themselves with assurance, with confidence, are perceived as dangerous—sometimes even to those in their own communities. Michael's brother sure looked dangerous to me, like he knew his way around a switchblade, but he also looked like he gave full rein to what might be called the expressivity of the individual Black body, moving himself through the world with a power, grace, and style calculated to bring the body into alignment with its own stylistic and expressive powers through sheer celebratory comportment.

Which left me and my brother in a conundrum faced by Black men everywhere. How could we, boys of intelligence, boys raised to be confident and self-respecting, go about without raising the specter of danger so readily projected onto our Black male bodies? How could we be ourselves, in step, happy, owning any given piece of pavement, any given city block, without being pathologized? Criminalized. Because a certain kind of white person is intimidated by even the slightest whiff of Black swagger, no matter how subtly it is deployed.

The Black church is one place, at least, where a certain kind of Black swagger can be both safely expressed and ritualized. Calvary Baptist Church in Jamaica, New York, afforded me plenty of opportunities to see Black expressive swagger in this most ritualized context, week after week. Here, within a sacred space, swagger took on the function of both expressing and transporting the congregation, giving us a sense of our own swagger and power. At some point in the sermon, the preacher would start inserting personal anecdotes, using his own experiences to illustrate the lesson at hand. Invariably there came a point in these sermons where the language skirted the colloquial, and the minister told yet another story of some slight that "the white folks" had tried to visit upon him. Drawing himself up and deploying his full oratorical powers, he let it be known that they hadn't been able to keep *him* in *his* place; his quiet grace and swagger had indeed seen him through the situation. And if those qualities had been sufficient to see him through, well, then, they must enough to get us through, too. And so we were primed to bring our own sense of swagger and inner power to whatever travails might confront us in the coming week.

But because I grew up firmly in the Black middle class, my own sense of personal and sartorial swagger was of a decidedly more muted kind, especially under the watchful and critical eyes of my mother and father. Their critique of the kinds of behavior likely to keep a Black boy from successfully moving through the world and toward a productive adulthood put little emphasis on outward expression while privileging the life of the mind and an outer life of decorum.

My brother and I were among the first group of Black kids to integrate all-white schools through busing; that is, we were taken out of the schools in our largely Black neighborhood and brought to schools in white neighborhoods, where presumably the quality of educational services being delivered was better. To survive in that world, especially in higher quarters, we had to become adept at what you might call a kind of behavioral code switching, the use of more than one language in speech. It soon became apparent that Black intellectual swagger was also suspect in such an environment, as I was constantly asked where I had copied my homework from, especially those assignments that required original thinking, such as writing a poem.

I was surrounded, though, by school friends for whom this was clearly not the case. Along with us Black middle-class kids who were bused from our parents' homes, there were those Black kids who were, literally, from the other side of the Long Island Rail Road tracks. These were the kids who showed up each day in stylish beaver-skin hats (stuffed with plastic bags to keep the shape), alpaca knit sweaters (tucked—just so—into the waist of their slim-legged pants), playboy shoes (which were brushed several times a day to keep the suede fresh), and swagger for days! Clearly, there was no one at home telling *these* boys to tone down the swagger. They were a walking, moving celebration of expressive possibilities, their language, style, and presence signifying a celebration of every pore of their being, their uniqueness in these precincts of conformity.

Swagger, then, is a clear act of reclamation, a way to both reclaim and celebrate viscerally an aspect of self that has historically been eroded. Certainly the history of the Black presence in America is a traumatic one: Basic ownership of oneself was painfully and forcefully transferred. Merely looking a white person in the eye was for a long time cause for the worst sort of retribution—at worst, death. So swagger can be seen as a way to reclaim and celebrate that which was forcefully suppressed, even as the deeper swagger—that inner sense of cool and self-assurance that is the deeper swagger—was never completely eliminated from our racial DNA.

The institution of slavery, wherein begins Black contact with the Americas, deeply encoded a set of relationships designed to eliminate all vestiges of Black humanity and place the Black body in a subservient role of utter subjugation. Along with this, a visual culture emerged to support and further reinscribe this role of disempowered servitude. Thus were Blacks depicted in visual culture as foot-shuffling, watermelon-eating, buffoonish caricatures, their very humanity stripped away. Whether in films, in which docility was the main role for Blacks, or in the posters advertising grotesquely pantomimed minstrel shows, or in children's books, where one would have encountered the happy and carefree little Sambo, there were precious few places where one would have encountered Black folks in all of their gloriously celebrated human complexity. While these images filled the public arena, Blacks always knew that those images were not theirs. And so the photographic image became important to the visual construction of Black humanity.

It was that urge to describe urban Black New York life through the camera that placed me in Harlem that long-ago afternoon, in the momentary presence of the stolid yet graceful Black woman and the carefree, swaggering Black boys. I had been inspired years earlier by my own initial encounter with the Black subject in photographs when I visited the Metropolitan Museum of Art at the age of sixteen to see the exhibition "Harlem on My Mind." That experience set me on the path to wanting to shape my own pictorial view of the African American experience. I guess you could say the camera became my own way of exercising my subjectivity in the world through persistant visual authorship.

As I watched those two boys walk powerfully into the expansive black space of the picture and into the late-afternoon shadow, and then froze that moment for posterity, I realized I was giving full and glorious rein to their youthful Black swagger . . . and my own.

PLAYERS
IN
ORDER
OF
APPEARANCE

HENRY LOUIS GATES, JR. is the Alphonse Fletcher University Professor at Harvard University, as well as director of the W. E. B. Du Bois Institute for African and African American Research. He is the author most recently of *Black in Latin America* (New York University Press, 2011) and *Faces of America* (New York University Press, 2010), which expand on his critically acclaimed PBS documentaries, and *Tradition and the Black Atlantic: Criticism in the African Diaspora* (Basic Books, 2010). He is the co-editor of *Call and Response: Key Debates in African American Studies* (W. W. Norton, 2011). His four-hour documentary, *Black in Latin America,* aired on PBS in April and May 2011.

dream hampton has written about music, culture, and politics for twenty years. Her articles and essays have appeared in the *Village Voice,* the *Detroit News, Harper's Bazaar, Essence,* and a dozen anthologies, most recently *Born to Use Mics: Reading Nas's* Illmatic, edited by Michael Eric Dyson. She was an editor at *The Source* in the early nineties and a contributing writer at *Vibe* for its first fifteen years. She coauthored the unreleased *Black Book* with Shawn "Jay-Z" Carter and collaborated with him on *Decoded.* dream is from Detroit and has lived in Brooklyn and Harlem most of her adult life. She publishes her name in lowercase letters as a nod to feminist author bell hooks, an early influence.

MAT JOHNSON is a novelist who sometimes writes other things. He is the author of the novels *Pym, Drop,* and *Hunting in Harlem,* the nonfiction novella *The Great Negro Plot,* and the comic books *Incognegro* and *Dark Rain.* He is a recipient of the United States Artists James Baldwin Fellowship, the Hurston/Wright Legacy Award, and the Thomas J. Watson Fellowship, and his work has been a Barnes and Noble Discover Great New Writers selection. Johnson is a faculty member at the University of Houston Creative Writing Program.

RACHEL M. HARPER is a writer living in Los Angeles. Her first novel, *Brass Ankle Blues,* was published in 2006, and her fiction and poetry have appeared in *Carolina Quarterly, Chicago Review, African American Review,* and *Prairie Schooner.* She has received fellowships from Yaddo and the MacDowell Colony, and recently adapted her second novel, *This Side of Providence,* into a television pilot. She holds a BA from

Brown University and an MFA from USC. Harper is on the faculty at Spalding University's brief-residency MFA in Writing Program.

Author **HELENA ANDREWS'** work has appeared in the *New York Times*, the *Washington Post*, *Glamour*, *Marie Claire*, and a bunch of other fancy places. Her memoir-in-essays, *Bitch Is the New Black*, is now available in paperback; Shonda Rhimes (*Grey's Anatomy*) is producing the film version for Fox Searchlight Pictures. In between penning screenplays and essays, Helena lives vicariously through every awesomely bad dance movie ever made, including, but not limited to, the *Step Up* franchise.

DAYO OLOPADE is a journalist and author of *The Bright Continent*, a book about African genius. She has written extensively on global politics, development, and technology in publications including the *Atlantic*, the *American Prospect*, *Democracy*, *Foreign Policy*, the *Guardian*, the *Nation*, the *New Republic*, and the *Washington Post*. She holds degrees in literature and in African studies from Yale University, where she currently reads law, in hipster glasses.

VALORIE THOMAS was born in Los Angeles and grew up in the Crenshaw district. She has a PhD in English from UC Berkeley and an MFA in screenwriting from the UCLA School of Theater, Film and Television, and is an associate professor of Africana studies and English at Pomona College in Claremont,

California, where she teaches Afro-Futurism; Literature and Film of the African Diaspora; Indigenous Knowledge and Aesthetics; and Literature of Incarceration. She has published and performed poetry and blogged for the *Huffington Post*, and is currently writing a book on diasporic vertigo. She is pretty sure the world would be better off if we would just *make. it. funky.*

For over twenty years, **MICHAELA angela DAVIS** has explored the power of beauty, urban style, women's politics, and hip-hop culture. Her magazine career began in 1991 at *Essence*, where she worked under her mentor, Susan L. Taylor, as fashion editor. In 2004 she returned as executive fashion and beauty editor and launched Take Back the Music, a multimedia campaign bringing awareness of the hypersexualized representation and lyrical disrespect of young women of color in mainstream media. She became the first fashion director of *Vibe* and *Honey* magazines, and also served as editor- in- chief of the latter. As a fashion stylist, Michaela has added her fresh fashion flavor to a host of magazines, from *Vanity Fair* to *Ebony*, and worked with artists and icons including Oprah Winfrey, Beyoncé, Maxwell, Diana Ross, Alicia Keys, Mary J. Blige, Prince, and Björk.

bell hooks is a down-home sophisticate, a Kentucky country woman. Just working always, reading everything, a distinguished professor of Appalachian studies. High priestess of love, writer of words to live by, more than twenty books, read by everyone, everywhere. Can heal and redeem. Claiming that cool is forever the only way to be and become.

VERONICA CHAMBERS is the author of several books, including *Mama's Girl, Having It All?, Black Women and Success,* and *Celia Cruz: The Queen of Salsa.* She most recently edited the *Glamour* cookbook *100 Recipes Every Woman Should Know.* She lives and cooks with her family in Hoboken, New Jersey.

MARGO JEFFERSON is a New York–based cultural critic. She won a Pulitzer Prize in 1995 and published *On Michael Jackson* in 2006. She's written and performed two theater pieces and is working on a second book. She teaches writing at Columbia University and Eugene Lang College. Looking back, she feels she has spent too much time being a Good Negro Girl and not enough being a Willful Negro Eccentric.

HANK WILLIS THOMAS is an artist working with themes related to identity, history, and popular culture. He received his BFA from New York University's Tisch School of the Arts and his MFA in photography, along with an MA in visual criticism, from California College of the Arts (CCA) in San Francisco. Thomas has acted as a visiting professor at CCA and in the MFA programs at Maryland Institute College of Art and ICP/Bard and has lectured at Yale University, Princeton University, the Birmingham Museum of Art, and the Musée du Quai Branly in Paris. Thomas's work is in numerous public collections, including at the Whitney Museum of American Art, the Brooklyn Museum, and the Museum of Modern Art. Thomas is represented by Jack Shainman Gallery in New York City.

STACEYANN CHIN is a spoken word poet, performing artist, and LGBT rights political activist. Her work has been published in *The New York Times,* the *Washington Post,* and the *Pittsburgh Daily,* and has been featured on *60 Minutes.* She was also featured on *The Oprah Winfrey Show,* where she shared her struggles growing up homosexual in Jamaica.

ULLI K. RYDER, PhD, is an award-winning educator, consultant, writer, editor, and thinker. She facilitates discussions of gender, race, ethnicity, identity formation, and media to foster diversity and create open dialogue. She is a full-time faculty member at Simmons College in history and Africana studies and has been a visiting scholar at Brown University. Like many of her generation, she grew up Black: the child of a white mother and a Black, white, and Native American father. She also grew up Buddhist, listened to copious amounts of jazz, Mozart, and hardcore punk, and believes her musical choices might explain a lot about her worldview.

MILES MARSHALL LEWIS has been an editor at *Vibe*, *XXL*, and BET and written for the *Huffington Post*, *Salon*, *Essence*, the *Believer*, and many other publications. He is the author of the novel *Irrésistible*; a biography on Sly and the Family Stone, called *There's a Riot Goin' On*; and *Scars of the Soul Are Why Kids Wear Bandages When They Don't Have Bruises*, a collection of essays. He lives in Manhattan. Instead of the more predictable Coltrane, Lewis named his youngest son Kalel, after Super-

man, the last son of Krypton. MML blogs at his site, www.
furthermucker.com.

ESTHER ARMAH has worked in print, radio, and television
in the United Kingdom, United States, and Africa for more
than a decade. She has been a journalist, investigative reporter, documentary filmmaker, and radio host for the British
Broadcasting Corporation (BBC), a London correspondent
for *Essence* magazine, and a contributor to the *Guardian* and
West African magazines. She has written four plays, including a one-woman show, called *Can I Be Me?*, adapted from her
book of the same title. Armah's play, *SAVIOUR?*, debuted at
the Dwyer Cultural Center in Harlem in 2011. Esther hosts
the fabulously popular *Wake Up Call* on New York's WBAI,
99.5 FM, every Monday through Thursday from 6:00 to 8:00
AM, and brings the posse together on her eternally popping
Facebook page, where a lively discussion is always in play.

DAWOUD BEY is an artist and writer currently based in Chica-
go. His photographs have been widely exhibited in museums
and institutions throughout the United States and abroad,
and are included in the collections of such institutions as the
Art Institute of Chicago; the Addison Gallery of American
Art; the Brooklyn Museum; the Museum of Modern Art,
New York; the National Portrait Gallery, London; the San
Francisco Museum of Modern Art; the Walker Art Center;
the Whitney Museum of American Art; and the Museum of
Contemporary Art, Chicago, and more. His critical writings

have appeared in publications throughout the United States and Europe, including *High Times Hard Times: New York Painting, 1967–1975*, *The Van DerZee Studio*, and *David Hammons: Been There Done That*. A recipient of fellowships from the John Simon Guggenheim Memorial Foundation and the National Endowment for the Arts, among others, he is currently a professor of art at Columbia College Chicago.

ACKNOWLEDGMENTS

It is impossible to thank all of the people whose energy and support made this book possible, but I will try.

Thank you to Jennifer Walsh at William Morris Endeavor, who thought the idea for this book was cool the moment I mentioned it. Thanks to Erin Malone, also at WME, who tweaked drafts of the proposal and worked tirelessly to find the right home. Thanks to Denise Oswald who thought the idea was genius, bought it, stoked it, and transitioned it smoothly over to Team Counterpoint. Thank you to Howard Yoon, who came to the meal a little late but brought lots of flavor.

Thank you to Roxanna Aliaga, who helped edit essays with the swift skill and discerning eye of a pro. Thanks to my publisher, Charlie Winton, for believing in the book and supporting it through publication and beyond. Many, many thanks to Laura Mazer, executive editor extraordinaire, for her generous spirit, patient camaraderie, thoughtful attention to detail, and tactful approach to deadlines. Kudzu!

Thank you to Henry Louis Gates, Jr. for his ongoing Black brilliance and humbling generosity. Thank you to all of the cultural workers changing the landscape and discourse of African and African American art and aesthetics, especially those who have supported my work over the years and this project directly. Thank you to Laylah Ali, Candida Alvarez, asha bandele, Jamyla and Pierre Bennu, Bliss Broyard, Stanley Crouch, Junot Diaz, Joel Dreyfuss, Shane Evans, Thelma Golden, Kellie Jones, Sasha Frere-Jones, Catherine Mckinley, Joan Morgan, Mark Anthony Neal, Melissa Harris-Perry, Jock Reynolds, Jason Samuels, Danzy Senna, Greg Tate, Kara Walker, Vera Wells, Deborah Willis, Imani Uzuri, and Colson Whitehead. The rest of you are in the book. Thank you.

Thank you to friends, students, and colleagues who have been such an essential part of my life and creative process over these last few years, especially Sena Jeter Naslund, Kathleen Driskell, Richard Goodman, and the rest of the family at the Spalding Brief Residency MFA Program. Thank you to the two photographers who have provided beautiful mirrors over the years, Amanda Marsalis and David Fenton. You inspire me.

I send endless lollerlove and gratitude to my assistant and start-up partner Lily Diamond, and a proud, gentle, affirmation to Rory Brill.

As always, I thank my readers. Your hunger to evolve keeps all of us who toil in our studios fed and watered, materially and psychically. You are so, so cool.

And finally, I thank my family. You know who you are. Without you, none of it would be possible, or worth it.

ABOUT THE EDITOR

REBECCA WALKER is an award-winning author and lecturer. She is the author of the memoirs *Black, White and Jewish* and *Baby Love* and editor of the anthologies *To Be Real, What Makes a Man*, and *One Big Happy Family*. Her writing has appeared in *Bookforum, Newsweek, Glamour, Marie Claire, The Washington Post, Vibe*, and *Interview*, among many other publications and literary collections. *Time* magazine named her one of the most influential leaders of her generation. A recipient of the Alex Award from the American Library Association, she has been featured on *Oprah* and *Good Morning America*. Visit her at www.rebeccawalker.com.